Table of contents
INTRODUCTION ....

    A sluggish industry 3
    A pillar of our society 5
    A revolution is underway 10

CHAPTER 1 - INVESTING MORE DIRECTLY 16

    Risk in real estate 16
    Colossal financing needs 19
    Flawed financial markets 24
    Direct contact between borrowers and lenders 28
    Facilitating mortgage-application process 37

CHAPTER 2 - INDUSTRIALIZING CONSTRUCTION 41

    Growing production costs 43
    Biomaterials for a greener construction 47
    Affordable acquisition of data 52
    Digitization of the construction process 54
    Off-site construction revolution 60
    On-site automation and robotics 67

CHAPTER 3 - REINVENTING PROPERTY MANAGEMENT 72

    Increasing market liquidity 74
    Easing the rental management burden 91
    The evolving role of asset manager 102
    Moving to predictive maintenance 106

CHAPTER 4 - MAKING THE USER A PRIORITY AGAIN 114

    A limited consumption 116
    Building As A Service 120
    Building As A Community 126
    Building As A Hub 131

CONCLUSION 136
AUTHORS 143

INTRODUCTION

Everything has been digitalized. Yet, the phenomenon remains very modest compared to what has really changed our lives. Even more than the digital revolution, urbanization is the most striking phenomenon of the last century. Let's consider some numbers. In 1900, less than 1/10 person lived in a city. Nowadays, a staggering half of the population does. By 2030, there will be an additional one billion people living in cities. By 2050, this number will reach three billions. 417 cities already host over one million citizens. Of those, 36 gather over ten millions. This number represents an astonishing one in six humans on the planet. Obviously, where there is a high concentration of people, there is also a high concentration of wealth. By 2030, 2/3 of the global wealth will be produced by 750 cities concentrating over one million inhabitants. In the words of Wellington Webb, former Mayor of Denver, "The 19th century was a century of empires, the 20th century was a century of nation states. The 21st century will be a century of cities."

Big numbers such as these can appear a bit abstract. Picturing 10 million people is no easy feat. The city itself however, has a tangible reality. A city is made of buildings and grid infrastructures. Urban considerations aside, it is important to underline how much time we spend inside buildings. According to a recent study, we only spend an average of 2.5 hours per day outside buildings. One hour of this time is also spent on public transport. That humans are sleeping inside buildings is not a new. We have done so for millennia. However, in the last century, technological progress in the agricultural sector led men to also work inside. Real estate plays a central role in our lives.

A sluggish industry

Alas, this real estate sector we are so reliant upon is stagnant. It remains so, in an era when technology creates revolutions in entire sectors, for the benefit of consumers and the environment alike. The public transport sector is undergoing a mutation with the development of ever less polluting vehicles. Soon it will go even further, with the appearance of autonomous cars, which will prevent thousands of accidental deaths. Energy production is becoming more sustainable thanks to renewable energies, with ever lowering prices. Agriculture will take on the challenge of having 4 billion more human beings to feed, whilst reducing the water and fertilizer needed. There are four major sectors catering to basic human needs - moving about, eating, keeping warm and having light. Real estate is the odd one out. Buildings are as expensive as ever to build. Living conditions do not change. Improving the quality of existing buildings is too expensive. The market is stuck to the point it prevents people's mobility.

Real estate is plagued by productivity stagnation, information asymmetry and high transaction costs. Real estate was a myriad of local, fragmented markets, without any economies of scale and with little competition. As a result the stakeholders involved have not been sufficiently encouraged to innovate. It eventually diverted essential resources to finance the deployment of the rest of the economy. We are suffering from a full-blown cost disease. "Cost disease" is an expression of the economist William Baumol to designate the differences in changes in productivity between different economic sectors. A string quintet nowadays still requires five people to play. The productivity of a music company is no different today than it was in Wolfgang Amadeus Mozart's era. Yet, within the same timeframe, factories have seen major productivity gains and are still improving. The time it takes to assemble a car has been divided by two between 1995 and 2003. It has been divided by two again since then. We now see this cost disease, which was confined to the arts or education sectors, showing in real estate.

At the heart of the issue is an extreme imbalance in supply and demand. The world's urban population has been rising by an average of 65 million people a year over the last three decades. Everyone wants to live in metropoles. Not only to obtain one's slice of the good life but also to take advantage of the opportunities for social advancement they offer. This is the reason why real estate prices are as sky-high from San Francisco to Shanghai, as they are in London, Moscow or Tokyo. Shanghai's per capita living space is 284 square feet (24 sqm), Beijing is 242 (22 sqm). This explains why the average statistics on real estate at the scale of a country have stopped making sense. This concentration in cities means land has become the rarest product in the world.

Some governments have taken steps to cool real-estate markets, tax on idle land and value gains, limitations on foreign- and second-home ownership, tighter rules on mortgages, housing subsidies, social housing or rent control. Real estate is heavily-regulated. National and local authorities impose construction standards. They define safe dwellings and give their vision of modern buildings with regard to performance as well as aesthetics. They also secure transactions, specialize land, finance consumers as well as producers. Bureaucrats' imagination is limitless. At the end of the day, housing policies represent 2% of the GDP in France, and 1.8% in the United Kingdom for mediocre results. Where we expect government intervention is making land available, promoting high-density housing and removing anti-competitive barriers. An industry is not unproductive by nature. It becomes unproductive due to the lack of innovation. Make real estate an engine for global growth is still possible. The solution does not lie in more regulation, but in more innovation.

A pillar of our society

This is all the more disastrous as real estate has been at the very heart of our economy for centuries. There is relative stability in the sector's importance. This is despite different national characteristics on a global scale, different estate rates, the heterogeneous maturity of economies, how old populations are, and the mobility of the work market. Our research has shown that along the retail sector, the real estate sector (including construction) has the most stable economic weight in OECD countries. This encompass economies with profiles as varied as the United States of America, European countries, Australia, Japan, Mexico or Chile. Over the last three decades on a global scale, the sector has been representing about one sixth of wealth creation. Consulting firms like Global Construction Perspectives and Oxford Economics took a more extensive approach and included construction materials and maintenance. Thus they predicted that by 2030, construction will account for 15% of global added value, against 12% today. [1] As the sector generates few or no gains in productivity, the prices of goods and services are not declining. This is in stark contrast to the drop in prices of other sectors, such as electronics. As a result, real estate represents an ever-increasing share in the most developed economies and in the budget of households. In Western countries, we spend more than 20% of our budget on housing and this number is growing. Collectively we are agreeing to always pay more for goods whose overall quality is deteriorating. Indeed, the weak renewal rate means the general improvement brought by new buildings barely compensates for the obsolescence of old buildings.

---

[1]Global Construction Perspectives & Oxford Economics, Global Construction 2030, November 2015, p. 6.

As a consequence of its economic weight and its inefficiency, real estate is predestined to be the sector where crises are born. We witnessed this at the beginning of the 1990s, or during the 2008 subprime crisis. It becomes a natural receptacle for liquid assets when a country is growing. Let us remember at the beginning of the nineties when land in Ginza 4 Chome district in Tokyo was reported to have traded at US$ 120,000 per square foot (US$ 1.3 million per sqm). This situation leaves investors ruined when the bubble explodes. It has been calculated that residential properties in the most high-standing neighborhoods were worth only one-hundredth of their value at peak time. China is famous for its ghost towns, whose real estate development projects remain desperately empty in the old industrial areas where the steel mills, cement plants and coalmines are at a standstill. Using queries on its search engine, a research team of the Internet giant Baidu has identified 50 areas in which residential real estate was unoccupied. They cite the case of Kangbashi, a neighborhood of 300,000 people built in 2006 in the city of Ordos to accompany the growth of the coalmines. Today, it seems that only one residence in ten is occupied. [2] Carried away by its own weight, real estate drives interest rates as much as it suffers from them. Due to its size, even in a difficult situation, central banks are tempted to adjust their policies in order to avoid abrupt

---

[2] Guanghua Chia, Yu Liub, Zhengwei Wua & Haishan Wua, Ghost Cities Analysis Based on Positioning Data in China, Big Data Lab, Baidu Research & Institute of Remote Sensing and Geographic Information Systems, Peking University, 2015.

recession effects. However, the impact of interest rates on real estate prices is challenging, since the demand for housing still widely exceeds the supply.

Real estate is not only an economic sector. By which we mean it is also strongly imprinted by social and cultural representations. Becoming a householder has long been an ideal to reach for in many societies. First it was seen as a show of social climbing, as well as a legacy. Later, as life expectancy increased and the work market became more uncertain, it became the assurance to have a roof whatever the situation. Governments still prioritize it. In the U.S., the federal government dedicated nearly US$ 143 billion to homeowner subsidies more than the entire budgets of the Departments of Education, Justice and Energy combined. The mortgage-interest deduction accounted for the biggest chunk of the total, US$ 75 billion. The two government-sponsored enterprises (GSE) Fannie Mae and Freddie Mac were founded following the Great Depression with the purpose of securing the financing of home mortgages and raising levels of home ownership. Loosening the monitoring of loan access conditions between 2001 and 2007 contributed to the rise of subprimes. The U.S. government had to commit to backstop the two GSEs with up to US$ 200 billion in additional capital in 2008 as the organizations had been accepting poor quality collaterals for mortgages. The recent Tax Cuts and Jobs Act (TCJA) as introduced some, limited, changes in the public support to home ownership. Prior to the act, a taxpayer could deduct mortgage interest for a qualified residence on the first US$ 1 million of acquisition debt and the first US$ 100,000 of home equity debt. Acquisition debt is defined as a loan used to buy, build or substantially improve a qualified residence. Any other mortgage debt is home equity debt. The TCJA lowered the threshold for acquisition debt from US$ 1 million to US$ 750,000 and repealed the deduction for home equity debt. Late 2015 in the UK, the Conservative party initiated a plan aiming to help one million households to become home-owners by 2020.

Universally, home ownership assistance policies are strongly criticized for their inflationary impact on real estate prices. On a macroeconomic level, many studies have explored the idea of a correlation between a high rate of tenants and a low unemployment rate, arguing that owning a property prevents geographic mobility. Yet they are still pursued for their symbolic value. Due to the large quantities of savings it receives, the real estate sector reflects strongly intergenerational exchanges, through inheritance and redistribution. It is the economic sector with the closest relationship to society, notions of solidarity over time through inheritance, and space through the distribution of social wealth. The increase in real estate capital value is questioned by Thomas Piketty as a symbol of growing inequalities. [3] The example of Yang Huiyan seems to support this view. The shares belonging to the heiress of Chinese real estate group

---

[3] Thomas Piketty, *Le Capital au XXIe siècle*, Le Seuil, 2013.

Country Garden have increased by 24% during the month of January 2018, earning her US$ 6 billion in ten days. However, economists proposed that the increase did not come from home equity revenues, but from the rise of real estate prices over this recent period. [4] Real estate capital, calculated as a sum of discounted rents, has remained stable in the U.S., the UK, Canada and France.

A revolution is underway

Innovation is not a dirty word in real estate. Historically, the sector even underwent a technological revolution in the 19th century, when modern cities were built. The sector saw great gains of productivity then. In 1818, Louis Vicat, a young French engineer, made Portland cement. Joseph Aspdin took out a patent in 1824 for this product. A few years later, in 1845, Isaac Johnson made the first modern Portland cement by firing a mixture of chalk and clay at much higher temperatures, similar to those used today. The same year, Pierre-Joseph Fontaine invented the modern lift, which became popular when American Elisha Otis took it across the Atlantic. During the late 19th century, the use of steel-reinforced concrete was being developed simultaneously by a German, Gustav A. Wayss, a Frenchman, Francois Hennebique, and an American, Ernest L. Ransome. In 1909, Thomas Edison received a

---

[4] Odran Bonnet, Pierre-Henri Bono, Guillaume Chapelle & Étienne Wasmer, *Le capital logement contribue-t-il aux inégalités ? Retour sur Le capital au XXIe siècle de Thomas Piketty,* Département d'économie de Sciences Po et LIEPP, Working paper n° 25.

patent for the first long kiln for cement. In the interwar period, French Eugène Freyssinet patented the much more resistant pre-stressed concrete, indispensable to the building of skyscrapers. After WWII, new techniques and new materials allowed an incredible reconstruction effort across Europe.

Another huge transformation is about to happen, driven by three factors. Firstly, software and hardware technologies together are turning real estate value upside down. A few of those are known and operational already, ranging from Building Information Modeling to blockchain, from drones to IoT. A myriad of young companies are now combining these technologies to reach new economic models, likely to generate real productivity gains. Also, public and personal data are collected in increasingly large amounts, and made available. Thus, today it is possible to know the prices and characteristics of properties, as well as urban regulations, for free. The third factor, which is probably the most important, is cultural changes. The sector is still very conservative, due to social or cultural representations associated with real estate. A parallel with the automobile can be made. As owning an individual car used to symbolize social status, conservatism in this sector did seem very important. Before the great recession, car manufacturers' CEOs still stated a car was a special, non-temporal good. The obvious presence of annuities, with tough barriers to cross, can be added to this cultural conservatism, rooted in a strong attachment to people's safety. Yet, this all changed very quickly. Firstly with a more standardized car production, coupled with a more fluid market, offering various options benefiting the consumer. Then, the focus shifted, from goods to service consumption. Within the next few years, we will witness the advent of autonomous vehicles, as well as the wider availability of vehicles producing no greenhouse gas emissions. This means paying for the miles travelled only, cost depending on how green the transportation is, will become a possibility. It will be an alternative to having an individual vehicle.

Millennials is perhaps the most overrated word used in real estate. People born after 1981 are said to change everything. Renters for life. Australian real estate mogul Tim Gurner even advised them to put their avocado toast toward a deposit for down payment instead. But numbers show they are not that different from their parents. In the U.S., millennials are even the most numerous real estate buyers today. 80% of U.S. and 75% of UK millennials who do not own a home intend to buy in the next five years, according to recent HSBC Group research. In Asia, up to 70% of Chinese millennials have their own house. Up to 91% of them plan to buy property within the next five years. However, if the same desire to own still exists among younger generations, it is seen more as a well thought-out decision to consume or invest than a symbolic rite of passage to adulthood. It is because ownership still has more benefits than rental in many countries.

Let's take a moment and look at this in a little more depth. Most people make a basic Return on Equity calculus. Homeowners in all 50 states and Washington, D.C., pay from 33% to 93% more for housing each month than do renters living in the same state. The difference plus the down payment required to buy a home, which is traditionally 20% of the home price for conventional mortgages, could be invested in the stock market. And finally, at the end of your mortgage, you compare the net value of your home and the value of your investment portfolio. Too often homeownership will win. But the right calculus to make is Return on Capital Employed. Real estate is LBO for Main street. Especially when you can deduct mortgage interests. In contrast, it is very hard to borrow money to invest in the stock market. Home equity line of credit just represents 3% of total household debt.

If homeownership is still attractive, real estate is becoming a commodity. In other words, it becomes a good, stripped from its historical and cultural heritage, and freely exchangeable in a transparent and competitive market. Owners, and even occupants, are ready to rent, exchange, share, let travelers stay, or store goods for others. In addition, the rotation of the housing stock is accelerating. Americans already move about 11 times in their lifetime but Europeans and Canadians move only 5 times. These figures will probably increase in the coming years. If a low quality client experience could be tolerated every ten or fifteen years, it is unacceptable every five or seven years. The ongoing revolution will start with paying more attention to customers. They're thirsty for personalization, and more likely to switch, a habit acquired from financial and telecommunication services.

The evolution of technology is turning it from the unusual to ubiquitous, so much so that there's hardly an industry that does not feel the disruption. Some sectors are embracing these changes quickly, BioTech for the health sector, FinTech for finance, AdTech for advertising, InsurTech for Insurance, and also EdTech for education. These represent sector mutations worth hundreds of billions dollars. Now, Real Estech (real estate + tech) is having its day. The objective is simple: moving away from real estate driven by constraints forcing people to adjust their behaviors to fit a limited offer towards a real estate responding to people's real needs.

The entire value chain is concerned: real estate, financing, construction, management and occupancy. For these reasons, Real Estech brings together PropertyTech and ConstructionTech. The cost of capital brought by investors, the cost of construction work, intermediary and building management fees, as well as occupancy fees paid by users, will drop and finally allow the sector to move upmarket. Productivity gains will allow cheaper and better quality construction, benefiting the consumer, the investors, and the sector's employees - whose work conditions are often still tough. Customer-centricity and zero-defects quality have spread across many sectors. Yet today, the imbalance between supply and demand in housing is such that consumers tolerate a service quality which would be unacceptable in other industries.

No citizen can escape this mutation: buildings are part of our everyday lives, either for housing or work. Some assets have already started to change - notably warehouses transformed by Amazon, or Airbnb competing with hotels. However other assets, such as housing, seem to be stuck in the Stone Age. Yet commercial properties only represent US$ 30,000 billion on a global scale, against US$ 160,000 billion for residential properties.

CHAPTER 1 - INVESTING MORE DIRECTLY

The first step in the asset lifecycle is the financing of its construction. Whether it is a residential or commercial property, a 50-storey high building or an individual house, no construction can be done without prior funding. Putting aside capital is always necessary in order to acquire land, and cover bills for the duration of the project (architectural studies, materials, workers' wages, etc.). Developers as well as individuals are aware of this obligation. In the end, the cost of capital represents a significant part of the total cost of real estate production. And in a world where new construction needs are huge, the funding issue is central.

Risk in real estate

Each real estate asset has a life cycle. Between the inception and the occupancy time, each stage offers different opportunities for investors based on capital requirements. Investment strategies are often divided into four investor profiles according to their appetite for risk and return expectations: opportunistic, value-add, core plus and core. *Opportunistic* represents those who come early into the project, those who invest their money before the start of the activity, or when the activity was interrupted and no profitability is guaranteed. Alternatively, more reasonable stakeholders (*core*) perceive modest regular incomes on stable assets.

Between those two options, there are investors who will accept some risk to improve the occupancy or the management, with a view to increase returns (*value-add*), or more simply, to find new tenants with some modest work (*core plus*). Financing major renovation of a real estate asset could be as risky as financing new construction. Renovation sometimes means a change in the function of the building, for example when an office building is turned into a residential building. The intent is to create an asset that did not previously exist.

Although it is often seen as a sector of unproductive people with a fixed income coming from their properties, the financing of real estate also has its risk takers. They forget that Baron Haussmann would not have been able to change the face of Paris, had it not been for the support of Émile and Isaac Pereire, Jewish bankers of Portuguese origins, who provided the necessary funds for urban planning. [5] They forget that if today the founders of Evergrande, Wanda or Country Garden are Chinese billionaires, they owe it to their role in developing modern Beijing, Shenzhen, Shanghai, Tianjin or Suzhou. The invested capital is considered risky, as many hazards do exist, especially finding tenants or buyers. The iconic Empire State Building in New York perfectly illustrates the risks. The American businessman John J. Raskob raised more than US$ 40 million before the 1929 crisis (equivalent to US$ 570 million today), in order to finance

---

[5]Emile and Isaac Pereire, *Bankers, Socialists and Sephardic Jews*, Helen H. Davies, Manchester University Press, 2015

the construction of the skyscraper. However, he was never able to rent more than 50% of the building surface. The Empire State Building was then nicknamed the Empty State Building, and was sold by John J. Raskob for only US$ 34 million. [6] There is no return without risk.

Real estate developers and individuals need financing. Developers have generally a negative working capital requirement. Many years sometimes go by between the initial investment of the developer (mainly the acquisition of the land and the construction expenses) and its future revenues from the sale or rental of the asset built. The number of administrative permissions, the heaviness of the work and the complexity of the marketing are the three main reasons for the duration of this portage. Developers have three sources of financing: their own funds, bank debt and presales. In the latter case, the final buyer also acts as financier. The respective importance of these three sources depends heavily on the country and the type of asset. The burden of debt is a lot higher in France and in Germany than it is in Spain. There, more personal funding compensates for the shortfall. For residential properties, in Europe and in Australia, presales are common and they can finance up to half of the funding requirement. In the U.S., presales dropped dramatically during the 2007 crisis, but have increased again since 2011.[7] The components of the capital cost are the interest rate offered by the bank, as

---

[6]David Farber, Everybody ought to be rich : the life and time of John J. Raskob, Capitalist, Oxford University Press, 2013.
[7]Once Again, Floor Plans Are Making the Sale, nytimes.com

well as the opportunity cost of the contribution made by the individual - the return given up by investing in future housing. By extension, they are accounted for in the cost price of the property. In the case of a detached house, the presale is a larger share of funding still. This precision is not insignificant as one in two Europeans, and two of out three Americans, live in a detached house.

Refinancing real estate consists of investing in the present. This means investing in an asset that is already built, either to draw a benefit as an occupant, or to ensure a fixed income from the current tenants. The underlying asset is then measured at market value, the operation contains little added value, and its financing is easier. Most of the issues about refinancing related to property management and particularly its sale, will be addressed in Chapter 3.

Colossal financing needs

In developed countries as well as in emerging countries, the existing housing stock is not adapted to the users' current needs. This is valid for residential properties, offices, and even commercial properties. Consequently, the need for investment in new built or in renovation has never been so urgent. Worldwide, McKinsey Global Institute has estimated that some 330 million urban households currently live in substandard housing or stretch to pay housing costs that exceed 30 percent of their income. This number could rise to 440 million households by 2025. [8]

In emerging countries, urbanization will make two billion humans move from the countryside to metropoles. The need for new housing is blatant. The demographic explosion, together with urbanization and the emergence of a middle-class, requires a huge investment in housing. Without this effort, the ongoing economic development is at risk of falling short. To picture the stakes, know that China produced 6.6 gigatons of cement between 2011 and 2014, when the U.S. used 4.4 gigatons between 1900 and 2000. This means China produced an extra third, thirty-three times as rapidly. [9] 40 out of 47 cities with the fastest population growth rate are in Asia whereas 20 of them are in China alone. According to the UN, in the course of the next fifteen years, the daily requirement for new housing will amount to 100,000 accommodations. This is in order to face the rural exodus, and improve the inhabitants' welfare. Vaclav Smil quotes studies showing that cemented interior floors are a decisive sanitary improvement, causing an 80% drop in parasitic infections. Kenya for example, needs 200,000 new accommodations per year, but only produces 50,000. The Ivory Coast however sets the record, with only 10% of satisfied demand. The need to produce many cheap

---

[8] McKinsey Global Institute, *Housing affordability: A supply-side tool kit for cities*, October 2017

[9] Vaclav Smil, *Making the Modern World: Materials and Dematerialization*, Wiley, 2013

accommodations falls within the scope of often neglected urban planning. The need for malls is also unfulfilled. CFAO, an important retail player in Africa, plans to open a hundred malls within the next ten years. Other emerging countries are opening to tourism, with a need to build hotels and leisure resorts.

In developed countries, this need to renew the supply is just as pressing, driven by two phenomena. The first is the requirement to reduce the energy consumption of buildings, which currently represents over 40% of total energy in Europe, and one fourth of greenhouse gas emissions. The second is changing lifestyles. Separate living arrangements are becoming the norm, due to the decline of the number of marriages, children leaving, and the growing number of separations. The consequence is a drop in the number of people living in each household. In the 1960s in the U.S., 3.3 people lived in each household, against only 2.5 in 2016. In Japan, this figure went from 3.5 to 2.5 during the same period. In France, by 2030, the number of households is set to increase 2.5 times faster than the amount of people. From a spatial point of view, economic activity feeds on ever increasing exchanges, implying a geographic proximity. Activities are therefore more concentrated in some strictly delimited spaces made denser, i.e. metropoles.

These trends accelerate the obsolescence of the existing housing stock, while the quantitative needs are on the rise. In New York City, Mayor Bill de Blasio announced in

2014 his commitment to reduce the number of homeless people by building 8,000 units of social housing per year between 2014 and 2021. [10] Since then, he has amended the plan to add 100,000 new social housing between 2022 and 2026. [11] Demand for this type of accommodations is very strong, to the point public authorities received 60,000 applications when 110 new accommodations opened in Fall 2017. MGI estimates that 1.5 million households cannot afford the cost of a decent apartment in the city. In California, in the city of Los Angeles alone there is a shortfall of at least 30,000 homes. MGI found that California added 544,000 households but only 467,000 net housing units from 2009 to 2014. In France, an objective to build 500,000 new accommodations was set in 2006 and never achieved. The increase in Parisian households would require 70,000 accommodations per year to be built, barely half of this achieved. In Germany, experts estimate the amount of new accommodations needed yearly at 350,000. This number will increase as the country welcomes refugees. [12] Many countries have public or semi-public housing systems, with capped prices in order to ensure population diversity. However, the moderate rent accommodations supply was mainly built from the 1950s until the beginning of the 1980s, and has been stagnating since. In the history of humanity, building

---

[10] "Mayor de Blasio's Plan for Affordable Housing", The New York Times, August 11, 2015

[11] "De Blasio Says City Will Hit Affordable-Housing Goal 2 Years Early" The New York Times, October 24, 2017

[12] Savills World Research, « Germany Residential Investment Market », February 2016.

on a large scale happened only after wars and the subsequent destructions they brought. Northern America, Europe, Russia, have not seen conflict on their soil for half a century. We are facing an unprecedented building exercise during peace time.

The situation is similar for other real estate products. The existing offer in developed countries is not adapted to the new demand. In the office property sector, new ways of working mean a new organization of space. Existing buildings may be redeveloped. Sometimes, this adjustment is not possible and the solution lies in new construction. In the retail industry, e-commerce competition forces the mall operators to rethink their processes. Everyday, customers go into shops, try a product, then go home to order it online. This also touches the hotel sector, with Airbnb being a game changer. It is essential to build new hotels, more adapted to the customers' demands. Aging public services buildings such as schools or medical facilities require new investments. All of these buildings are forced to adapt to face population ageing. By 2020, the number of disabled elderly will reach 60 million in the U.S., 80 million in the EU, and 80 million in China, using WHO's International Classification of Impairment, Disability and Handicap.

The real estate offer is rigid by nature. Building takes time, which creates imbalances on the market when demand soars. Today, an inefficient financing market compounds this inherent rigidity. The capital needed for construction remains a rare and expensive resource.

Flawed financial markets

First, it is important to differentiate two types of markets for construction or renovation. There are the very big assets, office or retail, often located at the heart of metropoles, and worth hundreds of millions or even billions dollars, and for which capitals are intermediated, which means they may come from financiers who are very far from the physical asset. The second type are traditional properties where financing is often ensured by local stakeholders, often located in the regional or national perimeter of the asset. The latter is often flawed and inefficient.

In developed countries, equity usually represents 20% of the total amount invested in a real estate development operation. Out of this 20%, the developer must himself bring about half, and has to find co-investors for the 10% remaining. This market financing by equity is characterized by multiple asymmetries of information, as well as barriers to entry. In the absence of a unified market, when a developer is looking to raise equity, he turns to a small circle of close investors. The ability to syndicate a pool of investors is reduced, so entry tickets are naturally high. As a consequence, little oligopolies of investors are born. The analysis of investment opportunities is often lead in a superficial manner. For lack of comparative data, the financing structure of the operation is very traditional and does not use the whole range of potential instruments. In the end, all of this automatically increases the cost of capital. When a developer does not find the external capital needed, he must himself invest the entire equity, restricting the amount of projects he intends to lead simultaneously. Access to equity is a major constraint in developing countries. A large amount of atomized and unorganized developers are left to their own devices. In Niger, which in 2019 will welcome the Summit of Heads of State and Government of the African Union, the construction of many hotels is currently halted due to a lack of capital.

Financing operations through presales, notably in the context of residential buildings, is also being questioned. For the buyer, it means taking a decision today, when it will have consequences in two or three years. Yet, with more convoluted lives and careers, planning is more problematic. Buying an asset to occupy it becomes increasingly difficult as people are more mobile. The mechanism which requires commitment, sometimes over years, before being able to acquire an asset, is getting harder to combine with the occupying acquirers' expectations. This encourages developers to solicit more and more individuals, who will then rent the asset. However, marketing expenses are very high, and therefore raises the cost of capital. In France, selling a new apartment for rent often represents 9 to 11% of its final price. In December 2017, a law was passed to limit this to a maximum of 7%. Furthermore, to encourage acquisition, financial incentives to buy-to-rent an asset have been put into place in many countries. There again, their impact is criticized as they tend to artificially raise prices. Also, the current weakness of borrowing rates for individual buyers does not come from a bigger efficiency in the allocation of banking credit, but simply from central bank policies. In the U.S., the average time to obtain a loan is still 40 days, and the management cost about 7,000 dollars.[13] If new brokers have appeared and are creating competition for the banks, their use has not become widespread.

Since the easy debt financing of the final buyers and the developers could become a substitute to equity, developed countries currently seem immune to this phenomenon of increasing cost of capital. However, the question is starting to surface in line with the end of central banks' expansive monetary policies. The banks will tighten credit conditions, putting an end to three decades of continuous decline. The average interest rate of mortgage loans in the U.S. has indeed followed the exact same evolution as the rate of government bonds, from 10% in 1990 to about 3% in the 2010s. This move is complemented by a stricter regulation since the 2008 financial crisis. With the Basel Agreements III, the regulators wanted to prevent the banks from repeating past mistakes. They are expected to lend less, while asking for more equity than before, as well as higher pre-sales rates. Finally, let's also underline the

---

[13] Fortune, *Blend Wants To Approve Mortgages In Minutes Not Weeks*, January 2016

directives imposed by regulations. Indeed, the new rules from the Basel Committee on Banking Supervision aim to secure the situation of banks which award long-term fixed rate loans, like mortgage loans. These directives, known as Basel IV, ask of the banks, which loan at a fixed rate over a long-term but refinance themselves in the short-term, to better protect themselves in the event of a potential raise of historically low rates. This targets European banks in particular, as they keep loans in their balance sheets and often loan at a fixed rate. Their Anglo-Saxon competitors sell the loans back on the financing market and lend at variable rates more often. Since these banks cannot afford to raise their equity again, the consequence would be a reduction of the volume of mortgage loans granted. When finance tightening starts, small operators with a more entrepreneurial profile will have difficulty in finding financing. Such a situation can be seen in Spain and Italy, where the difficulties of the banking sector already penalize real estate development.

Such an inefficiency is valid in the refinancing sector. An individual wishing to invest in real estate products must often go through a long chain of intermediaries to reach stakeholders with a limited knowledge, a restricted investment mandate, and high management rates. When he prefers to invest in listed stakeholders, he also faces restricted investment strategies on which he often is passive. The active investor must therefore often invest directly in assets, which is very time-consuming and creates considerable barriers to entry. Indeed, to invest, it is necessary to acquire an entire asset, which often represents a considerable marginal investment.

For the most qualitative real estate assets, the financing mechanism is different. It is a lot more efficient. Assets allocation is ensured by professional stakeholders. They mobilize equity directly with institutional investors, have a better knowledge of opportunities, and are more capable of assessing them. Private equity real estate funds play a key role in the functioning of this market. Their names are Carlyle, Colony, Blackstone, KKR or also Tishman Speyer. They use powerful analysis tools, benefiting from the experience of thousands of already completed transactions, as well as from multiple types of financing tools, they can syndicate investor consortiums and even face financing markets if necessary. However, these funds often have a mandate restricting the type of assets and the investment's geographic position, as well as a lifecycle rarely exceeding eight to ten years. In the end, this type of financing remains very limited in the total of new constructions.

Direct contact between borrowers and lenders

Beyond the exogenous impacts of central banks' monetary policies or tax incentives from the States, many new innovating stakeholders really want to improve the allocation of capital. Many startups on the border or Real Estech and Fintech already bring lasting solutions to improve communication between borrowers and lender. Digital is indeed turning the classic financing chain upside down through the creation of two-sided platforms. From the point of view of the investor, these (i) reduce intermediary costs, (ii) split the entry cost, (iii) widen the scope of potential investments and (iv) reduce the asymmetry of information. From the point of view of the developer, they (v) speed up the constitution of the financing and (vi) reduce the weighted average cost of capital. These distribution platforms will contribute to erase the distinction between more qualitative assets for which the financing is already efficient, and more traditional assets. What we saw on financing markets in recent years with a democratization of access will happen in real estate too.

Crowdfunding was initiated in 2003 by the ArtistShare platform. Mainly intended for jazz musicians and composers, ArtistShare works like a music label, allowing the creator to finance his project with the support of the audience. In this case, members of the community donate to the artist they support. Since then, crowdfunding has been supporting all kinds of projects, from artistic production to startups, as well as humanitarian projects. In 2015, the global crowdfunding industry reached a never seen before level (US$ 35 billion), of which a significant part was directed towards real estate financing (US$ 3.5

billion). [14] Applied to real estate, it means that developers come to find the funding they need directly on a crowdfunding platform. In this sector, there are no donations. Investors deliver loans or potentially take shares in the capital of an ad-hoc structure created specifically for a particular operation. In the U.S., the first platforms were created in 2011. Due to higher interest rates and less presales than in Europe, the model is thriving there. Among the pioneers, RealtyMogul relied on a community of 80,000 people who invested US$ 200 million in total in 300 different projects selected by the platform. Many developers thus found the adequate financing to develop residential and commercial products. Crowdfunding was used to finance a symbolic project: the 3 World Trade Center, third highest building in New York. Some platforms have a higher range positioning and target as a priority the richest individuals under the form of club deals. It is the case for CADRE, a startup co-created by Jared Kushner, Donald Trump's son-in-law, who raised US$ 65 million in June 2017. In total, more than 100 platforms are active in the country.

From Canada to Australia, and from Asia to Europe, the model of real estate crowdfunding is taking off, and communities are getting bigger. Online crowdfunding platforms like Duocaitou focused on hotel and apartment projects are gaining momentum in China. There are more than 130 crowdfunding platforms in the country, but the

---

[14] Massolution Crowdfunding Report 2015

most mature stakeholder of the area is CoAsset, a Singaporean company introduced to the market in 2016. France is the first market of the Eurozone for real estate crowdfunding with more than US$ 110 million in 2017 against 65 million in Germany.[15] [16] Developing countries are also riding the wave. The platform Realty Africa is present in most sub-Saharan Africa, and relies on a network of 100 local developers. The investors are mostly members of the African diaspora who want to invest in their country. Initiatives have also launched in South America. In Colombia for example, a 787 feet (240 meters) high skyscraper christened the Bogotá Downtown Bacatá, the first skyscraper in the city in 35 years, was financed by a large crowdfunding campaign of US$ 150 million, the biggest campaign known to this day. On the global scale, over US$ 3.5 billion were invested in 2016 through real estate crowdfunding platforms, of which about 2 billion were in the U.S., and 1.2 billion in Europe. The progress margin is huge when we know that investments going through American crowdfunding platforms only represent 0.3% of total investments in the country today.

The first positive impact of crowdfunding platforms is to reduce intermediary costs. Until now, there were many

---

[15]*«Crowdfunding immobilier : 2017, l'année de tous les records »*, Les Echos, December 2017

[16]*"German Real Estate Crowdfunding Market Booms"*, Crowdfund Insider, June 2017

intermediaries between the agents with a financing ability, and those needing financing. In the old model, banking and insurance brokers sell investment products to investors. These funds are centralized at the level of regional or national headquarters, then a dedicated team is in charge of reinvesting them alongside developers looking for a financial partner. All these stakeholders receive compensation in the process, thus the cost of capital is higher. In France, an investor who puts some of his savings in a real estate investment trust (REIT) must pay 10% fees for the subscription, as well as annual fees of around 2%. On the other hand, platforms often charge very competitive management fees, usually limited to only one fee, around 8% at the time of raising the funds. Digitization alone does not explain these reduced costs. The amount of investments realized by the platform also plays a part. When most of real estate investments trusts only complete a few operations per year, platforms do a greater amount of smaller ones.

For an individual investor, many projects become accessible. It is not compulsory anymore to buy a whole unit, but rather a fraction of the project is thus securitized. Some platforms like Property Moose offer minimum tickets for 13 dollars. They give access to many geographic areas, and to a whole range of real estate projects, from residential to services. The ability to diversify one's portfolio and reduce risk is much stronger. Investors can thus take positions in different cities in the same country. Why buy a whole apartment in New-York?

Instead you could buy 25% of this asset, 25% of an apartment in San Francisco, 25% of another in Detroit and 25% of another one of same value in Miami. The risk is therefore better spread, and impervious to the evolution of local markets. This can also be done with investments in foreign countries in order to benefit from the economic dynamism of those countries. The growth of crowdfunding platforms in Australia is explained partly by the appetite of the Australians for real estate investments in Asia.

Financing development operations is by nature risky. However, there are also rental investment crowdfunding platforms. An investor may buy part of a rented asset and receives rental income. With a minimum investment of US$ 500 in Fundrise or US$ 1,100 in Brickvest, you can choose exactly which projects you want to put your money by getting access to real estate opportunities that were historically unavailable to most people, portfolios of student accommodation or retail leases. Each investment is given a rating to help investors find opportunities that match their own risk profile. Each investor can then build a balanced portfolio from home, without having to deal with greedy intermediaries.

Many meta-platforms have been launched, giving investors access to all operations open to financing on all the platforms in the country. AlphaFlow is one of those platforms flourishing in the U.S. The company raised US$ 4 million in September 2017, notably with Point72, the family office of Steven Cohen with US$ 11 billion assets managed. This way AlphaFlow offers investors to multiply small tickets in various operations. The platform also makes available a rather sophisticated follow-up tool, which for example can generate a diversification indicator.

Finally, the platform gives access to analysis tools. They used to be reserved for professional investors only. The core business of the platform is to choose the best projects carefully, the selection ratio being about one for ten with RealtyMogul. Crowdfunding platforms can generate increasing returns with economies of scale. Here, each project financed through the platform enables to better measure the risk of a future operation. Growth leads to efficiency. For example, the platform can compare estimated prices provided by the developer with the selling prices actually applied during the operation. The same analysis can be made concerning the costs of work. The platform refines in real time its knowledge of the real estate market and increasingly appreciates the risk inherent to each development operation. This promise of efficiency convinced the first institutions to invest through crowdfunding platforms rather than relying on external teams. The large asset manager Direct Lending Investments thus committed to invest US$ 73 million in the projects offered on the real estate crowdfunding platform Realty Mogul. The market is currently concentrating, which shows the expected scale impact. In July 2017, the RealtyShares platform, after funding more than 1,000 operations, acquired Acquire Real Estate. The new group will be able to rely on a community of more than 120,000 American investors. Other consolidation operations will happen in the upcoming months.

From the developer's point of view, participative financing enables to raise funds quicker. Indeed, the velocity of circulation of capital was also suffering from the multiplication of intermediaries. The English platform Property Partner pulled off the feat to raise US$ 1.2 million in less than 11 minutes. Although this case is incredible, a developer finding the required financing in a few days only is not a rare occurrence. The platforms also bring a sorely lacking transparency to the financing market. In the past, big developers with a long history could obtain all available funds. The trend is changing. Developers with more entrepreneurial profiles now have access to capital. More generally, this new financing source enables developers to put less equity in each project, and thus to raise the number of simultaneous projects. The cost of capital is between 8 and 12% for the borrower. The banks, which originally did not welcome these platforms with open arms, now see real estate crowdfunding as an additional financing source.

However crowdfunding platforms are as much an opportunity as a fatal threat to developers. A reconstruction of the very fragmented real estate value chain can be conceived, due to the bigger circulation of information. Let us consider the example of development opportunities. Until recently, investors thought that only the developer knew how to identify free and interesting properties. He therefore accepted to pay this knowledge. Startups like Envelope in the U.S. or LandInsight in the UK now scan and update local urban plans, making this information readily accessible. Their tools enable the quick identification of available plots corresponding to specific criteria, such as proximity to subway or building surface. The Envelope software even generates various architectural scenarios in order to help the operator visualizing the opportunities offered by one given plot. Better still, participative financing platforms can rely on their community to do this research work. Investors also appreciated the developer's expertise on a given market. Tomorrow, platforms will use their abundance of data and will be able to know markets better than developers will. Therefore, what is the developer's role in this new value chain? In the U.S., the company Prodigy Network is both a crowdfunding platform and a real estate developer. Vertical integration enabled the company to raise more than US$ 150 million to develop projects in New York and South America. Asset managers could also be tempted to move up the value chain by relying on crowdfunding platforms. In France for example, the French hotel group Maranatha finances the construction of its new facilities through the Look&Fin platform.

Facilitating mortgage-application process

Simultaneously with the advent of crowdfunding, bank financing for real estate developers is becoming more efficient. While the lending trade is still too often reliant on Excel spreadsheets, new tools enable banks to better assess the repayment capacity of the borrowers. The startup CrediFi specializes in this type of tools and provides multiple data to bankers for each development operation they intend to finance. In addition, the software easily fits into Salesforce, the world leader in customer management tools. Based in New York and Tel Aviv, CrediFi already raised more than US$ 23 million to ensure its development. One of its competitors is Built, a startup created in 2014 that also raised US$ 20 million. The latter goes even further by helping banks to follow the progress of the work they fund. Indeed, all concerned parties (developer, builders, banks, investors, etc.) access a single platform and interact. The banker can follow the project and also propose adjustments or heavy corrections. 35 banks have already worked with Built for a business volume of over US$ 6 billion since 2015.

The financing of individuals' real estate projects is also mutating. New stakeholders help banks interact with their clients. The American startup Blend has a software to facilitate mortgage loans requests by reducing the processing time to a few minutes. The financing brokerage market has also seen new players appear, like Habito in the UK. Here again, the aim is to modernize the old financing brokerage business. The company claims to analyze in real time over 70,000 loan offers from 70 different banks, and helps their clients find the best offer. Habito founders have developed this matching tool because they feel that about 25% of borrowers do not choose the optimal solution for them, with an average additional cost of 5,500 dollars. Habito has raised US$ 25 million in September 2017. Trussle, a competitor of Habito, was elected startup Proptech by Tech City News for 2016. The latter has signed a partnership with the Zoopla sale platform in September 2016. The buyer can find the property that suits him and an adapted financing without leaving home. The process also works the other way. Indeed, Trussle informs its clients on their debt capacity, allowing them to ultimately define the budget they want to devote to the acquisition of the property. Sometimes, these new players are banks themselves. Sindeo, established in 2013, grants loans to individuals after a few minutes long online application. Rocket Mortgages, launched in 2015 as the face of Quicken Loans' online mortgage application, enables a prospective purchaser to know precisely the maximum loan he may contract. Honk-Kongese startup WeLab operates Wolaidai, one of China's leading mobile lending platforms. In January 2016, WeLab completed a US$ 160 million Series B fundraising round. Chinese Huifenqi mixes online mortgage application and property management tools as most of users look at getting a mortgage for a rental property. Crowdfunding is also a source of funding for individuals. Thus, there are many two-sided platforms where individuals contract loans with other individuals in order to finance the construction of their house. This is what the RealtyShares platform offers. Financial innovation seems limitless. Landed, Patch Homes, Point Digital Finance and Unison are new companies experimenting shared-equity contracts as an alternative to cash-out refinancings or to help new buyers with a down payment. Future homeowners get money for part of their down payment in exchange for pledging some of the home's future price appreciation. The length of the contracts can vary from a few years to 30 even if homeowners can repay early.

By capturing data from multiple clients, the platforms always know more about their ability to repay. We are witnessing the advent of "smart capital", or how to make financing smart. Such platforms are all the more gaining traction as banks seems stuck with old financing models, regardless home mortgage are based on assets in European countries or based on income in U.S. As our friend Nicolas Colin said *"To date, banks have not developed products beyond granting credit for buying a home to households with savings and a high probability of a stable, single-sourced income in the future. Despite their purportedly high knowledge of the risk profile of their customers, banks are unable to guarantee rent payments to a landlord or attribute a high credit score based on an individual's future earning power in an age marked by permanent instability and frequent career shifts."*

*   *   *

If the upcoming joint reduction in the cost of capital and construction is great news, it carries with it a complicated equation. Automatically, it will have a deflationary effect on the price of the goods. Thus, the current real estate investors would see their portfolios lose value. They would therefore be limited in potential new investments, not to mention the possible systemic risk. It does ask the question of how fast the decline in real estate prices will spread, from newly built to old buildings, in the event of intense reconstruction accompanied by a densification of the land to better adjust supply and demand.

CHAPTER 2 -
INDUSTRIALIZING CONSTRUCTION

The building trade stands out from other markets by its very long product cycle. The buildings have long life spans, although these tend to slightly decrease. According to the U.S. Department of Energy, the average office building lifespan in 2008 was 73 years. In contrast, human life expectancy in the U.S. was 78 years. In other words, it is necessary to separate what constitutes first production from what is part of the renovation. The importance given to renovation compared to new construction often reflects the image of a sluggish real estate sector. It translates the reluctance of political leaders to change the urban landscape, even when it appears beneficial to the public interest.

Construction is probably the most regulated segment of the real estate sector, both from the point of view of the new standards for construction and planning, and regulation of local urban planning, restricting the density or the destination of the property. The weight of the regulations is such that some manufacturers prefer to strip a building and renovate it fully, although it costs more than a simple demolition and reconstruction, to avoid being subject to the new regulations. Average car longevity is 12 years, but nobody would think of renovating the existing car population for conversion to electric mobility. For reasons as symbolic as political, demolition is the exception where it should be the rule. Demolition technologies are controlled and cheap – around 10 dollars per square foot approximately (110 dollars per sqm). Yet, in Europe they are often reserved to large groups of buildings built in the 1950s and 1960s on the outskirts of big cities, which have become urban ghettos with derelict housing. If this situation is particularly true in Europe and to a lesser extent in the U.S., it is inherent to the degree of development of the country. These considerations have long been ignored in Asia but they emerge today in cities like Hong Kong, Singapore or Beijing where the preservation of the heritage has become a strong demand of public authorities.

The preservation of heritage is desirable but has social and economic costs. They should not be overlooked. When Baron Haussmann destroyed a large number of historic buildings to develop the modern Paris, he did not hesitate. Many were opposed to these changes. In 1852, Victor Hugo himself was upset by the transformation of the city and wrote so in an article entitled "war on the destroyers". [17] If today the buildings of the 19th century no longer meet the requirements of quality and performance, we should not hesitate either. What causes a dilemma between upgrading of old buildings and reconstruction, is often the issue of rehoming former occupants during the work period. The more construction will be fast and

---

[17]Victor Hugo, « Guerre aux démolisseurs », Revue des Deux Mondes, 1832.

mechanized, the more the inconvenience of the demolition and reconstruction will be minor.

Growing production costs

As we stated above, from a quantitative point of view, the construction needs are huge. Yet, producing has never been so difficult. Studies on the weakness of productivity gains in the construction sector are numerous and old. In the 1960s already, experts were worrying about the relative stagnation of the sector compared to the rest of the economy. The American Department of Commerce produced a report pointing to the slow acceptance of innovations. The situation has remained unchanged since then. In Sweden, for the 1993-2003 period, productivity gains in the construction sector were only one tenth of those measured in the manufacturing industry sector. A McKinsey study on two decades in France even established that hourly productivity in the construction sector experienced a decrease of 6% while it progressed by 87% in the manufacturing sector.

Several authors temper this judgment. They state that real estate incorporates innovations related to building materials. These innovations are not seen in the face value production, but in the value of building use, at the global level or at the level of individuals. For example, the development of polymers by the chemical industry has led to the arrival of materials such as Corian or Ayonite, more resistant and easier to maintain. They are used extensively in restaurants, hotels and hospitals. If this statement is correct, there are also many buildings for which the drop in the cost of construction has been more than offset by more maintenance or higher maintenance costs. Evidently, even though measurement instruments are less robust than for other sectors of the manufacturing industry, the pace of technical progress in the construction sector is low. To make an easy comparison, the Empire State Building and its 1,250 feet (381 meters), the world's tallest building for nearly 40 years, was built in 14 months, hiring 3,400 workers, five of whom lost their lives. Construction of the Burj Khalifa tower in Dubai, the world's tallest tower with 1,918 feet (584 meters), lasted 60 months, employing 7,500 workers at its peak, one of whom died.

Even though many sectors - banking, retail ... - invest heavily in their digital transformation, the construction sector seems to be stagnating. A 2014 study by JBKnowledge in partnership with the University of Texas A & M found that one-third of U.S. companies spend less than 1% of their turnover on computer and digital technologies. 40% of the companies surveyed did not have a dedicated IT department. Worse, among companies with more than US$ 500 million in sales, nearly half were below that 1% investment threshold. Gartner confirmed that the average spending in the construction sector for computer and digital tools stagnated at 1%, when it was over 3.3% in the rest of the U.S. economy. In terms of public and private R & D expenditure alone, they stagnated at 0.4% of the sector's annual output, five times less than the aeronautics sector, four times less than the automotive sector and half as much as the banking sector. These figures are found in Europe in neighboring proportions. The instability of the sector, hit by increasingly brutal crises and victim of the reduction of its margins, leave little means for innovation.

Part of the explanation lies in market dynamics. When demand is high, companies have little interest in innovation. The other part lies in the standards. Construction is the victim of strong regulations, setting very high standards. As long as they are respected, those standards allow the manufacturers not to be disturbed, but also lead them to ignore any notion of performance. There is no concept of performance in the building. Outside seismic zones, a building is too solid, whereas a structure such as a bridge or dyke can work to its physical limits. It's not just about safety standards, but also building quality standards such as the addition of overhead light fixtures or outlets above the worktop. Lastly, it is necessary to mention the multiplication of the elements aiming to improve the working conditions on building sites, which increase the global bill of construction.

Cultural factors may also explain this low investment rate in the future, including the preference for evolutionary rather than disruptive change, with tried and tested tools and technologies. It must be recognized that the lack of production is a vital risk, as was the case for car manufacturers. Thus, the slow diffusion of plasterboard is explained by the resistance of plasterers, accustomed to spread the plaster or coating finish by hand. Nor should the widespread belief that investments in new tools are not financially profitable be ignored. Finally, regulators are also quite conservative about the introduction of new products.

The structure of the sector is often put forward to explain the weakness of the investment. The proliferation of small enterprises operating in limited geographical areas and without vertical integration appears to be one of the main reasons for the inability to integrate, or even stimulate innovation. The barrier to the entry of the construction sector is weak. These occasionally erratic businesses do not have the capital resources to invest in modern tools and production processes. The cost of moving a workstation from 2D to 3D is estimated at around US$ 15,000. These small businesses lack the human resources to use the new tools or to innovate at the level of their profession. The training costs associated with increasing the skills of their employees may seem prohibitive. They are also difficult to reach for institutions that research or promote innovation.

The fragmentation of the sector is to be compared with the fragmentation of real estate operations. This is therefore part of the urbanization drive of the public authorities. The multiplication of small operations tends to fragment the ordering parties and make them more conservative in the introduction of innovations, whose cost could be better amortized over larger groups. It leads to a competition of costs at the expense of the quality of the project. The fragmentation of projects tends to prevent economies of scale associated with the development of a neighborhood, and on the contrary increases the costs of installing lifting equipment in dense areas. The preference for renovation rather than new construction generates significant costs.

In spite of these barriers to innovation, episodes of high increases in productivity show that construction is not doomed. Countries in which construction stakeholders invested massively in order to modernize their processes, such as Japan in 1980, drew a profit. Today, by revisiting old innovations with digital help, new stakeholders might be able to radically change the way to produce buildings.

Biomaterials for a greener construction

Innovation in construction starts with building materials. It has been concentrated in this sector for decades. A study showed that materials producers represent about two third of R&D expenditure in relation with real estate. Saint-Gobain spends more than 4% of its turnover on research and development. Fields of investigation and progress in this area are identified and known. Innovations are the result of very large companies that have experienced a phenomenon of concentration in recent years.

The innovations concern the development of new materials as much as the improvement of those already used. Advances focus on nanomaterials. It is now possible to create hybrid materials that add to the support properties. For example, memory or hydrophobic properties can be added to metal or ceramics. These materials will not be part of the structure of buildings, but will develop smart windows or heat exchangers. The first electrochromic glass production plant was established in the U.S. This glazing, which darkens by electric control, enables a total control of light and heat in the buildings. It is also now possible to industrialize the production of graphene, a material of great conductivity and resistance discovered in 2004. Research on elastic waves has made it possible to create materials capable of ensuring the diffusion of waves without altering their composition, notably making it possible to resist earthquakes. Coatings research will improve existing materials, be it glass, steel or even paper. Made of nanoparticles of titanium dioxide, they allow for example the repelling of water or dirt. 3D printed silicone metamaterials make it possible to create complete mechanisms in one piece, like a door latch with its integrated handle. Tiles and slates are also reinvented to integrate photovoltaic technology to the frame. This is the bet Elon Musk made with Solar City, producing slates in quartz, but also of French Imerys or Italian Dyaqua.

Other works are aimed at improving the star materials that are cement and concrete. The applied research work continues to add other materials that can make them ever stronger, lighter and more flexible, and less consuming in water by adding different nanomaterials. The Austrian company LiTraCon, which specializes in the creation of building materials, created a sort of translucent concrete into which optical fibers have been inserted. Developed by a team of researchers at the University of Wisconsin-Milwaukee, Superhydrophobic Engineered Cementitious Composite (SECC), it is much more water and crack-resistant than traditional concrete, with a lifetime that could reach 120 years old. One of its major assets is its ductility - the ability of a material to deform without breaking - that could be up to 200 times greater than ordinary concrete. Some innovative companies promise substantial reductions in the carbon footprint of concrete. Like the English Novacem or the German Celitement, the company Solidia Technologies aims to reduce by 70% the generation of CO_2 in the production of concrete. Several large groups including Total, Lafarge, BASF, BP and recently Air Liquide have invested in this company.

The construction revolution will come from the use of natural materials, notably wood. In order to succeed, it is necessary to further improve its resistance to moisture and its rigidity by progressive heating. Moisture resistance is increased by 30 to 50%, resulting in better durability and stability in the dimensions of the wood over time. Timothée Boitouzet, who was awarded French innovator of the year by MIT Technology Review, created his startup Woodoo in 2015 in order to make wood two to three times more rigid, rot-proof, waterproof, but also translucent. The method implemented is to remove the lignin of wood to replace it with a plastic of natural origin, which strengthens the molecular structure. Cardboard is a promising biomaterial. The American company, BetR-blok, based its activity on the design of brick from cement and cellulose from recycled paper and cardboard. Bricks have good strength, and are even very good thermal and acoustic insulating materials, while also being mold and fire resistant. Tests are being conducted on less known materials, such as flax or hemp.

Biomaterials are still in their infancy but their dynamics are very promising. Construction and new buildings will be increasingly valued in terms of their greenhouse gas footprint, including CO_2 footprint. Yet, the improvement of building energy performance means that construction, which previously accounted for only 20% of their carbon footprint, now represents half. The four modern building raw material production processes involve significant CO2 emissions: 1,800 kg of CO2 per ton of steel, 300 kg of CO2 per ton of glass, about 150 kg of CO2 per ton of concrete and 50 kg of CO2 per ton of wood. In addition, the emissions associated with the production of concrete today represent 6-7% of global CO2 emissions. The advantage of biomaterials is that, during their growth, they absorb some of the CO2 in the atmosphere. They also have a very strong potential for reuse, either by recycling the resource or by producing heat through combustion. As biomaterials are lighter, they also imply lower energy consumption during transport and assembly. Their lightweight also makes them ideal to build high buildings. Wood is still little used, with a few exceptions in Canada or the U.S., and in Scandinavia for individual houses, due to the abundance of the resource. The weakness of its use is explained by the lack of sector structuring whereas the markets of cement, concrete and steel are very concentrated. However, things are changing. Big producers of Cross Laminated Timber (CLT), veils of solid wood assembled with cross-folds which form bearing walls or floors with a power-to-weight ratio and excellent mechanical, thermal and acoustic performances, are appearing and are able to reduce costs. More and more builders are getting used to working with this material, sometimes complicated to use in wet weather, for example.

Some manufacturers like Katerra even integrated the value chain by building its own 250,000 square feet (23,000 sqm) mass timber manufacturing facility in Spokane Valley, Washington. The company raised more than US$ 1 billion, the latest round led by SoftBank's Vision Fund. It was co-founded by Michael Marks, the founder of Silicon Valley private equity firm Riverwood Capital, and former CEO of contract electronics manufacturer Flextronics. Marks was not a guy from the real estate sector but he knew what challenging an old industry means. In the end, more ambitious projects are created using wood, not only for the dressing but also for the structure of the building. In Chicago the construction of a 650 feet (200 meters) wooden tower is taking shape and Japanese timber company Sumitomo Forestry has revealed plans for the world's tallest wooden building in Tokyo, a 980 feet (350 meters) skyscraper.

Affordable acquisition of data

Feasibility studies prior to construction are still too long and too costly. Before launching the construction of a building, there is indeed an abundance of data to collect, whether it's regarding the size of neighboring buildings or the topography of the ground. This information requires measures, facilitated by new capture tools that promise significant productivity gains. For the exterior, new cameras like the Leica Geosystem's Pegasus allow scanning of the environment at nearly 80 mph. For the renovation of existing buildings, 3D laser test patterns enable the acquisition of several million points in a few moments, even if dregs of data have to be reprocessed (for example if a curtain hides a column). Google's Tango, a rear-mounted tri-cam device connected to an augmented reality computing platform, scanned the surroundings to create highly accurate representations used in real estate. It was not as successful as expected and Google scrapped Tango in favor of ARCore. Apple deployed its ARKit technology, turning iPhones into augmented reality machines. German NavVis is an important player in mobile indoor mapping and visualization. Munich-based startup reduce the cost of capturing and comparing data of physical structures to design models. It has raised a US$ 9 million Series B round of funding in 2015.

The use of drones with high definition photographic tools should also generate significant productivity gains. During the pre-work stage, they allow a finer mapping. During the works, they constitute the optimal solution for the control of the project's progress, in particular when the constructions are vertical and difficult to reach. This solution was initially reserved for professionals, but individuals could benefit from the drones' cost reduction to pursue their own projects. In San Francisco, the startup Skycatch enables its customers to pilot drones from an application: the drone goes on site by itself and takes pictures of the site. The photos are then available on the Skycatch site. Finally, the drones will be used to certify conformity at the end of construction, including covered and uncovered premises and energy performance. Here again, the time saved will be valuable and will reduce the total duration of a real estate transaction. Launched in 2013, the Identified Technologies startup uses autonomous drones to carry out such surveys and just raised US$ 1.5 million. From 2014, the French construction giant Bouygues offers data surveys by drones. The drone can take on average 80 points per square foot against 1 point every two or three meters for a geometrician topographer with a laser. H3 Dynamics, a designer of smart drones, joined the Singaporean GTC sponsor to develop a drone able to detect cracks in building façades. FairFleet360, a Munich, Germany-based startup, connects independent, licensed and insured drone pilots with construction firms.

Finally, databases or mapping tools are appearing, that collect all the data and store it to avoid repeat tests by several potential buyers.

Digitization of the construction process

Construction is a succession of tasks led by different bodies of work which implies high costs of coordination and a multiplication of the risk of error. Several studies have estimated between 25% and 50% of the waste was related to the coordination of tasks, moving, installation of tools and equipment, and verification of the progress of the construction site.[18] Digital tools, by their ability to aggregate data, analyze it quickly, and writing it in a form understandable by all, are source of huge productivity gains.

The elementary component has been the development of digital models, which include the geometric features of the construction as well as information on the nature of all objects used (composition, physical properties, mechanical, behavior, etc.). It can be in 2D or in 3D. These tools are gathered under the name Building Information Modeling or BIM. The information is in IFC ("Industry Foundation Classes") format, which enables interoperability between different software programs. First, these models generate significant productivity gains in the design phase by improving the quality and accuracy

---

[18]National Institute of Standards and Technology (SITC) ou Tulacz and Armistead (2007).

of records to study, and anticipating the problems to be solved. The impacts of architectural alterations can be simulated live from the point of view of building and regulatory constraints. This tool more easily enables the unification of the architectural gesture with the engineering of the building, saving precious time going back and forth between the architect and the design office. We saw some architects being hostile to the digital model because of the limitations it imposes on creation. Truth is, architects are often still paid on the total amount of the project, and do not have any interest in minimizing the cost.

The second benefit of BIM is the improvement of the marketing of real estate when it is in 3D. The model can be combined with virtual reality headsets, allowing end users to immerse themselves in the building and a life-size representation of the future building. The third benefit of BIM is precision. It enables cost transparency. Builders will no longer use approximate ratios and margins and will be able to get close to the exact amount of waste needed. Competitiveness will be equally enhanced. The fourth benefit of BIM is its scalability. A building site is a realm of uncertainty. The model initially designed by the architect can be used by each of the construction trades to obtain the necessary information, and in return is amended in real time based on his own achievement. Finally, its last advantage is to ensure the coordination of the different trades. It forces to anticipation, and therefore movement towards industrial methods with a time control granted to each task, methods known as "taktées" methods. For the construction of Tour D2, a 171-metre tall skyscraper in the La Défense business district, Vinci was able to organize work sites, structural steel and façade in cycles of 15 days corresponding to the realization of three floors, with tasks durations to the minute. The effects are substantial: some companies have managed to cut construction costs up to 40% on shopping centers with zero production flaws, allowing avoidance of extra work. The digital model also allows you to easily trace the responsibilities of each person, and to thus simplify the phase of removal of contingencies in case of dispute. At the end of the project, the model is the digital double of the building and becomes a valuable tool in the maintenance of the building, or even its renovation or deconstruction. This model could even fit in a neighborhood where the environment and adjacent buildings have also been modeled.

BIM modeling is now broadcast to large groups of building and public works, engineering and architectural firms. The pressure for the adoption of these tools is growing. Aware of the potential for innovation associated with the use of this work method, governments are launching initiatives to accelerate its diffusion. In its directives related to the award of public contracts, the European Parliament asked to integrate digital processes such as BIM to improve the effectiveness of trade in the stages of tendering and competition. Some governments have already structured national plans for the promotion of these tools. Thus, starting in 2011, the UK published a strategic report on the construction sector to generate at least 20% savings, and made it mandatory to exchange basic digital data as of January 2016 for all public contracts above US$ 7 million. In Finland, the U.S. and Norway, government agencies in charge of public buildings have widespread BIM respectively since 2007, 2007 and 2010. In Singapore, the objectives of public buildings using BIM were 100% as of 2016. Most importantly, a fund has been implemented to help stakeholders in the evolution of their working methods by taking over the costs of training, equipment, software. In parallel, improving Internet coverage, including in the most remote sites, assists in the diffusion of these technologies. The construction sector also recruits new generations of workers accustomed to digital tools in their daily lives, who do not understand why these tools should not available in their professional lives.

The major distributor of BIM solutions is Autodesk with Autocad. It is worth pointing out Graphisoft (ArchiCAD), Dassault Systems and Bentley Systems as main competitors. Nemetschek Group, Graphisoft parent company, and Trimble formed a strategic alliance in 2015 to expand the deployment of BIM across the entire lifecycle of buildings. Innovative companies are positioned downstream with coordination tools for building sites or. These Saas (software as a service) products are destined for small and medium-sized enterprises and are often based on less expensive and more accessible solutions in 2D. Among these tools allowing their users to store, follow the construction plans and sequence the work plan, we can mention the American PlanGrid and Fieldwire, which raised respectively US$ 58 and 13 million. Honest Buildings is an online construction project management platform for landlords and developers, allowing them to manage and solicit bids from contractors and oversee budgets. In 2017, the company raised US$ 13 million in a Series B funding round that included Brookfield Property Partners and Rudin Ventures. In Europe, French FinalCad helps to transform 2D plans in 3D plans, which are then used by workers on the construction site, for example to report defects during the reception of the work. The company has already raised US$ 25 million and has 100 employees. Brussels-based Aproplan, which bills itself as a "Salesforce for construction," is digitizing the construction industry, and has raised US$ 6 million in Series A funding. In Asia, Novade, a mobile application to streamline construction site processes and facilitates collaboration, is already used by a number of major builders such as Singaporean CapitaLand, Japanese Obayashi or Malaysian UEM Sunrise. Such software can then be linked to material supply systems to also manage the logistics and purchasing. In a more advanced version, one can imagine a real-time aggregation of data retrieved by equipment and workers in order to compare them with the wishes of the developer, and make an updated and shared work plan.

Other programs focus on the improvement of internal management of builders like the US$ 3 million-funded

Australian startup Assignar. Assignar's system allows a construction company to keep track of its workforce, assets and regulatory compliance, which are often done in spreadsheets. the software improves the business relationship between the manufacturer and end customers, especially for the tracking of changes requested during construction or for its reception. Finally, the data collection on projects to improve the maintenance of the equipment is developing, the same way it developed in factories. In December 2015, Caterpillar signed a very ambitious partnership with the big data startup Uptake, valued at US$ 2 billion, in order to exploit the mass of data the equipment giant collects on sites.

Yet once more, technology is colliding with the organization of the value chain. Industrial methods no longer need to size tasks depending on the size of the teams. Teams can adapt to meet the exact needs of the site, instead of adapting to the progress of the construction site a provider can achieve. This implies changes in the size of the teams, and therefore providers of a sufficient size to vary the available workforce. Yet a work site is still the place of intervention of a myriad of subcontractors of usually small size, whose reduced workforce cannot work with high load peaks that require industrialized production. Last but not least, the greatest variation in the size of the teams on a site requires having refectories and construction toilets adapted to this range of numbers. The fragmentation of the operators, and the weakness of their margins, does not allow them to bear the costs of investment and training in the digital model. In some projects the developer must pay for the upgrade of the entire supply chain to make sure he has a functional digital model, delivered at the end of the project. The multiplicity of stakeholders leads to the question of data ownership of the final model, the legal responsibility of different stakeholders, and the alignment of stakeholder interests.

Off-site construction revolution

The mechanization of production must meet the multiplicity of stakeholders, their heterogeneity and the misalignment of interests. It involves increasing the number of operations carried out off-site in a centralized space, capitalizing on the division of labor, the specialization tasks and the serial production. Various building elements are built in a factory and transported to a construction site. Off-site construction is not a new idea for developers and architects, but its usage is on the rise. Perfectly suited to dense urban areas, this mode of production made the building site go from a plant with a lot of negative externalities (footprint, noise, duration...) to a simple assembly site. This production would generate only 5% of waste against 20 to 30% for on-site construction, by dividing the number of errors by 20. The assets with redundancies such as student and senior housing, education buildings, hospitals are more suitable for off-site construction.

Buildings are not permanent. Like planes or cars, these are complex products made of various components, each with different life cycles. When the structure of a building is made to last a century, networks expire after 20 years, the interior after 10 years, and electronic components within 5 years, according to Professor Thomas Bock and Thomas Linner, authors of several books on construction robotics. [19] The integration of water, electricity, gas, and data networks within the walls is a real problem because the risk is a lack of upgradability. Practices evolve, as evidenced by our ever-growing demand of electrical outlets. The integration of networks and electronic elements in the permanent parts of the building make it extremely expensive to innovate, and generates a lot of waste. This is the case for those hotel rooms with integrated wall ports for iPhone, when connectivity has change. According to the American public environment agency, renovation contributes to 40% of the total waste of construction, as much as demolition itself. The solution is a new approach to construction, around a building divided between different subcomponents, sustainable structures in which modules could be integrated and removed after their expiry, while being reused elsewhere. These modules would notably target facades, water, electricity and gas networks, bathroom and kitchens, which include many elements integrated into the building.

---

[19]Thomas Bock & Thomas Linner, Robotic Industrialization : Automation and Robotic Technologies for Customized Component, Module, and Building Prefabrication, Cambridge University Press, 2015.

This would allow movement beyond the simplest renovation, which consists in repainting and changing the floors. The European Commission has funded a project, EASEE (Envelope Approach to Improve Sustainability and Energy Efficiency) to develop renovation modules for buildings built between 1925 and 1975 on the outside facades, walls and interiors. This path has been explored for a long time by Japanese companies of prefabricated buildings such as Sekisui House or Toyota Housing. These are looking at the building as a service to improve continuously, and offer gradual upgrade solutions. This approach is beginning to inspire new initiatives like Open Building Institute, which offers free online models of components. The goal is to reconfigure the apartments or offices whilst maintaining the structure of the building.

Modular production, in other words similar and replicable modules in large quantities, is also growing. Today, building standardization can produce entire modules enabling huge gains in productivity. A Chinese air conditioning installer, Broad Group, created a subsidiary to produce industrial buildings. The company has built a 6-storey building in a day for the Shanghai Expo, the Ark 15-storey Hotel in a week, the 30 floors T30 Tower in a fortnight and the J57 Mini Sky Tower of 57 floors in nineteen days. 90% of the structure is produced at the factory, including ceilings, floors and windows, plumbing, electricity, ventilation, and only the rest is built on site. It is, however, important to notice that the J57 Mini Sky Tower is currently unoccupied since its completion in

2015. Buildings such as residences for lone people (pensioners, students) lend themselves particularly well to this type of construction. As for car parks, Australian Parkd also bet on modular production, and raised US$ 6 million less than a year after its creation. A plant can store items to be delivered on a daily basis on-site, thus optimizing cost, with the limit of 3D module transport being more inefficient because it equals to moving vacuum.

In the context of individual habitats, modular production was originally a response to emergency situations. The Architects for Society (AFS) has thus designed the Hex House, made of isolated steel tubes and metal panels to be mounted by the end users. IKEA has also designed The Better Shelter Housing Unit, low-cost housing that can be mounted in six hours by 4 people, and dismantled when necessary with a lifecycle of three years. In the U.S., modular production is becoming fashionable, including amongst the largest housing manufacturers, as an answer to labor shortage. We know of the mini-houses - less than 500 square feet (46 sqm) - movement started in 1997 by Sarah Susanka, which has progressed in recent years. However, this mode of construction is now of interest to the biggest technology groups. Google announced a partnership with Factory OS in June 2016 for the construction of modular homes in Silicon Valley. This is to accommodate temporary employees who struggle to find affordable housing in the area where real estate prices are so high they curb the arrival of some talent. The order covers 300 modular homes for a total price estimated between US$ 25 and 30 million. Ten Fold Engineering, a British startup, has created a buzz online with its modular and portable buildings that spread out in less than ten minutes. The demonstration building measures approximately 700 square feet (65 sqm) and costs less than 130,000 dollars. Modular homes are built entirely in a factory and assembled on-site, reducing the cost of the construction from 20 to 50%.

Beyond the modular, innovative businesses offer pre-designed dry materials that allow for substantial gains in productivity on the job site. Created early 2015, Smart Cast aims to industrialize the construction of concrete floors for collective apartment buildings and single-family homes. The permanent form panel in fibro-cement, cannot be dismantled and is used as a coating finish and installation template with already built-in networks. This provides a time saving of about 10%. But other companies go further such as Katerra, whose numerical model is built from elements picked in an object library. These elements, wooden or concrete, are then directly produced in factory before delivery to the site for assembly. French Woodeum, the developer founded by Guillaume Poitrinal in 2013 ex-CEO of Unibail-Rodamco, advocates a similar model. These panels, prefabricated and precut at the factory, delivered by order of installation, enable a sequencing of tasks and track the work with a centralized software program. The design of the buildings has long been influenced by local cultures. This method combines different elements and produces different buildings. Thus it also answers the issue of architecture standardization. In fact, more and more prefabricated buildings are receiving architecture awards. The CitizenM Tower Hill was voted hotel of 2017 in the UK. However, standardization does not mean ugliness. Besides, Haussmann Paris is an example of extreme standardization which is still today highly appreciated.

Off-site construction still varies a lot across countries. In Netherlands one out of five new dwellings uses wood or concrete prefabrication, in Sweden it concerns more than eight out of ten detached houses and about one out of ten new residential building in Germany according to D. Steinhardt and K. Manley of Brisbane's Queensland University of Technology. In the U.S., the UK, France or Australia no more than 5% of permanent housing has any significant prefabrication but more and more players turn to off-site construction. In May 2017, Marriott International announced plans to modularly construct 13% of its North American developments. There are no less than 120 buildings in production in the UK. Manufacturer Laing O'Rourke has recently signed a partnership with developer Stanhope that could see US$ 2.8 billion worth of schemes developed using offsite methods over the next five years. Governments also play a very important role in the dissemination of these new modes of production. The city-state of Singapore is a model. The authorities progressively forced manufacturers to build off-site in order to avoid nuisances linked to the presence of building site on such a dense territory. In 2020, building bathrooms and toilet blocks in modular will be compulsory. Australia is also a pioneer, with many high buildings built off-site in Melbourne or Sydney. In Europe, the UK government took a resolute position in favor of off-site construction since the *Modernize or Die* review published in 2016. The Farmer Review of the UK Construction Labour Model was commissioned in February 2016 by the government. It investigated the current construction model and proposed actions to improve the industry's future. The UK government is to prioritize the use of offsite construction to improve the cost effectiveness, productivity and speed of construction delivery. Chancellor Hammond announced the state will spend US$ 60 billion in public procurement to drive the adoption of the technology.

From very dense Asian skyscrapers housing projects, to American suburbs of single-family homes, through hotels in restricted European cities, manufacturing off site is spreading everywhere. It relies on digital models and biomaterials to completely revolutionize production methods.

Digital is pushing the re-composition of the value chain and its integration, by simplifying the exchanges between the various stakeholders. Integrated and repetitive strategies will succeed to fragmented and project-driven organizations. Katerra is the best example, by having integrated creation, design, production of materials and their assembly. Even in cases where the prefabrication is only partial, a new model is appearing, close to that of an automaker with its outfitters. It then comes to agreeing with providers to record the transfers of value added. For example, for formwork panels with pre-installed electrical kits, the on-site electrician only has to perform a check. Logically, his remuneration should be adjusted, or is he the one who pockets all the added value.

On-site automation and robotics

Off-site construction will not answer all the needs of construction. New automation solutions are emerging as to achieve gains in productivity directly on construction sites. In recent years, three-dimensional printing, more commonly known as 3D printing, received a lot of hype. This mode of additive manufacturing was first used as a means of rapid prototyping by some industries handling specific parts, such as aeronautics or medicine. it is now becoming more widespread, and enables to fast design various objects with a biggest choice of materials.

3D printing can help with boosting creativity by opening up a world of designs and shapes previously unattainable or too time-consuming to realize by hand. Additive manufacturing in the building sector may result in better productivity and less waste material, as only the material put in place would be needed. but it is still at an exploratory research stage. This first attempt happened in the low-cost construction sector. The Italian company WASP for World's Advanced Saving Project has developed a 39 feet (12 meters) high 3D printer called BigDelta. The goal is to produce houses using local resources, including clay, and to consume very little power. Today, the technique is becoming widespread. The benefits of 3D printed buildings are obvious, since both labor savings and time savings are considerable. On top of reducing the cost price of the property, 3D printing is more ecological. Indeed, the delivery of equipment and materials to construction sites is optimized with this new technology. China is a pioneer in the field. Yingchuang Building Technique, Chinese producer of fiberglass structures, created a business dedicated to additive manufacturing, called WinSun. After building the first 3D wall as early as 2008, in 2014 WinSun succeeded to print 10 houses of 2150 square feet (200 sqm) in 24 hours, and with a single giant 98 feet (30 meters) long and 33 feet (10 meters) wide 3D printer. In 2015, they renewed the exploit by printing a four-stories building in 3D. The question that remains unsolved concerns the materials used by the printer. Initially, it was a mixture of cement and construction waste made of concrete, sand and glass, which led to a very low cost of US$ 5,300 per building, but the reliability of such a building was debatable. Since then, doubts have gradually disappeared, to the point that the Chinese company HuaShang Tengda, the market leader, claims that the buildings it prints in 3D can withstand earthquakes of magnitude 8. The company recently printed a two floors house of 4,300 square feet (420 sqm) in less than 45 days in Beijing, using 20 tons of particularly solid C30 concrete. The Xtree startup has developed a specific printhead for concrete placed on an ABB robotic arm. Technology has enabled the printing of a building approximately 215 square feet (20 sqm) in twenty hours with 700 coats of an experimental cement developed by LafargeHolcim. Control of the robot is done through the Dassault Systems' 3Dexperience platform, in order to select the optimal structures for the building and use only the amount of material needed. Israeli startup Tridom is attempting to develop a robotic platform, based on a Kuka robotic arm, incorporating important software developments to drive the robot despite external conditions. Other companies are emerging in the U.S. with Contour Crafting. 3D printing is very exploratory research.

The other big innovation aside from 3D printing is the automation of machines. The Australian company Fastbrick Robotics Limited has created a robot able to lay 1,000 bricks per hour at a rate four times higher than that of a human operator. Using a robotic arm guided by laser positioning indexes and 3D CAD software-driven, the machine is fed by bricks that are deposited on a treadmill, then coated with adhesive, before being affixed to each other. American Construction Robotics has created SAM for semi-automated mason. Such robots are far from standard use. It costs roughly US$ 400,000 and requires workers to load its brick, refill its mortar and clean up the joints. The Japanese are very involved in the automation of machines, especially to deal with the construction needs for the Olympic Games of 2020 while labor is scarce. Komatsu, the second largest Japanese construction group, launched an initiative called Smart Construction, designed to automate bulldozers remotely piloted by drones that provide real-time data on the ground. To do this, Komatsu uses Skycatch drones, in which the group has invested US$ 25 million. Kawada, another group of construction, is well-known for its HRP-4 robot that can carry equipment, install drywall panels, assemble steel tubes and even drive forklift trucks. Apellix, a startup based in Florida, has rolled out two products in 2017, a drone-based dry film thickness gauge and a painting drone.

*　　*　　*

Construction is probably one of the segments of the real estate sector in which the most important productivity gains are coming. Investments are considerable but could change the way we build. More capital could also mean less work. Given the weight of the construction sector in employment, in developed countries as in emerging countries, hundreds of millions of jobs could be threatened. However for some, automation is an answer for skilled labor shortages as the sector does not attract new generations and baby-boomers are retiring. Nearly two-thirds of bricklaying contractors say they are struggling to find workers, according to a survey by the National Association of Home Builders. Besides off-site construction provides workers with safer working conditions in a factory than out in the field.

CHAPTER 3 - REINVENTING PROPERTY MANAGEMENT

Once a property is financed then built, its owner must manage it. He may delegate this task to an intermediary, but the problems are always the same: sell or keep? occupy or rent? repair or prevent? Private owners as well as large management funds constantly arbitrate between these alternatives. The ownership involves one-off events (purchase, repair, etc.) while the occupation, dealt with in the next chapter, implies common expenditures.

Firstly, in many economy sectors, the preference for usership is progressively replacing the preference for ownership. The American essayist Jeremy Rifkin has been one of the first to theorize this shift in his book The Age of Access.[20] Philosophers will see a reaction to triumphant individualism in collaborative economy, where sociologists invite us to consider what time means to new generations. These arguments are correct, but they must be complemented by a more economy-based analysis. Indeed, the preference for ownership is also the consequence of more complex secondary services associated to the ownership of an asset, which leads to an increase in time and money charges for their selection and monitoring. Thus, for personal mobility, ownership of a

---

[20]Jeremy Rifkin, *The Age of Access: The New Culture of Hypercapitalism, Where all of Life is a Paid-For Experience*, Penguin, 2000

car now involves the support of ever more complicated maintenance with the widespread use of electronics, intermediate consumption, compliance with environmental standards and insurance requirements. The time when the layman could repair his car on his own is long gone. Consumers prefer a more complete and personalized offer rather than the composition of a package of services, with the benefits of time and money. Indeed, for now these packaged offers mainly concern the richest consumers, but they are starting to spread. This is how we went from owning a car to the consumption of mobility solutions expressed in miles, more or less expensive depending on the emission of carbon dioxide. When a product becomes a package of services, it is more easily exchangeable. This phenomenon is called commoditization.

This growing awareness starting to affect individuals already took place in the 1990s for a number of large companies. Today, big corporations should not have a real estate division. Real estate is too costly, and does not do well with the growth and recession phases a company might encounter. From an individual point of view, being an owner comes with its issues. Even today, the property owner is seen as a captive customer by a large number of producers of services he is forced to use. From real estate agents to rental managers, as well as condominium trustees and building architects, many professions suffer from a bad press from the point of view of the owners. Automobile regulators try to limit abuses, but some of the existing stakeholders easily go around new regulations, waiving them or integrating the legal risk in their profit calculations. Even worse, most of the devices implemented can artificially distort competitive relationships, with increasingly strong impacts. Faced with this, digital technologies allow the homeowners, individuals as well as professionals, to reclaim the management of their property in the sale, rental management and maintenance. Better management by the owners also means a better offer for tenants. Indeed, when the property becomes a burden, it is common for assets to be completely taken off the market. Digital technologies enable an increase in the available offers by making the latent supply visible, and to better match the demand.

Increasing market liquidity

After years of increasing speed of exchange for real estate assets, it has been stagnating since the great recession. In Australia, a real estate asset used to be held on average for 5 years in 2005, against 8 years in 2014. In the U.S., the figure went from 6 years in 2008 to 10 years in 2016.[21] In France, the holding period of old accommodations went from 9 to 7 years between 1999 and 2008 before going back up since. This increase of the holding period is not a choice. It goes against socio-demographic dynamics. This can be blamed on the crisis, but also on the archaism which today still characterizes a

---

[21] National Association of Realtors (NAR)

property transaction. Workers should be able to move in and out without hassle and without the upfront costs and occasional asset depreciations that go with frequently switching jobs and moving home. And yet, since the creation of online search portals at the end of the 1990s, few innovations have marked this segment. Since the acquisition or rental of immovable property remains episodic, consumers are looking for reassurance. Therefore, they are more readily going towards known brands, an advantage for former newspapers turned websites, or for physical networks with their windows used as advertising tools. This weak recurrence of the purchase or rental action also explains why the customers are ready to tolerate a mediocre quality of service. A more intensive use of existing technology will allow a better flow of real estate.

The residential and tertiary market are still much intermediated. Indeed, the action of purchasing or selling is very engaging, and as such the presence of many experts (real estate agents, surveyors, diagnosticians, architects, lawyers, notaries, brokers...) to advise or organize this very heavy process is reassuring for many customers. It is estimated at some US$ 50 billion in developed countries. The chain of operations of the sales process is more divided, and classic centralized intermediaries must increasingly resort to external service providers who each offer a specialized service. If most of the examples developed below deal with the residential market, they also apply to the shops and offices of small surface with a high supply and demand. Above a certain amount, the buyers and sellers are rarer, information cannot be shared, and intermediaries still have a crucial place.

The first challenge is regarding the advertisement content. The buyers, especially the youngest, are not content with simple pictures and now favor a virtual tour in 3D. The American startup Matterport, which has established partnerships in Europe and Asia, specialized in this niche directly selling its services to real estate agents. They take a 3D camera, the cost of which keeps going down - today they're sold for about US$ 250, and they deal with the capture. Matterport then does the modelization, and sends a finished product to the real estate agent, ready to use for marketing. It is no coincidence that the French startup Meero, specializing in real estate photography in Europe and in the U.S., raised over US$ 18 million in August 2017 with billionaires Xavier Niel and Bernard Arnault. Professionals will then be able to share pictures and videos of the assets on sale directly on social networks. The European developer BNP Paribas Real Estate created a pod allowing remote visits to buildings using virtual reality. For already built buildings, Asian developers or real estate agents can also use the new tool made available by the PropertyGuru platform. It takes pictures of buildings with drones, which also film the environment at the same time. Buyers therefore have a very precise idea of the view from a flat, without having to go there.

The publication of advertisements went from using small local dealers, to very concentrated super-portals enabling to reach a wide audience of potential buyers. The first digitization of the sector consisted in putting online the information that used to be found in newspapers. In 1995 already, the site Realtor.com was launched in the U.S. and competed with traditional press adverts. Today, 87% of American buyers do their research on the Internet.[22] 65% of millennials state they found their property on their mobile.[23] In France, 92% of property transactions began on the Internet. The scale impacts associated with such a platform leaves no doubt regarding the upcoming concentration of the sector. In the U.S., such a concentration has already begun with the acquisition of Trulia by Zillow in 2014 for US$ 3.5 billion. The new group relies on more than 160,000 million unique visitors every month. More than 180 homes are seen every second just on mobiles, and the database of the platform has 110 million accommodations, of which 67 million are currently on sale.[24] Massive centralized advertising portals such as Zillow, Rightmove or Zoopla vastly improve liquidity in the residential real estate market by connecting buyers with agents. Multiple Listing Services (MLS) which enabled horizontal sharing of inventory between agents are now replaced by a vertical interaction between estate agents and portals. Traditional real estate agencies are forced to use these platforms to publicize their offers. In

---

[22]Zillow Group Report on Consumer Housing Trends, October 2018
[23]National Association of Realtors, Home Buyer and Seller Generational Trends Report, July 2017
[24]Zillow, Reports Record Third quarter 2014

2017, Zillow eliminated ability for real estate agents to manually post listings in a move to put pressure on more MLS and brokerages to send listings directly to the company. Creating a personal portal is very expensive, and requires huge advertising investments but estate agencies have shown resistance to the inflating fees charged by large property portals. In the UK, in 2015, the main estate agency chains launched OnTheMarket.com to challenge the dominance of Rightmove and Zoopla. The site forced agents who use it to choose between the other two instead of listing on all three. In February 2018, OnTheMarket has been listed in London with a market value of about US$ 138 million. In France, the largest real estate agents networks have co-invested to develop their own platform Bienici to compete with SeLoger, the dominant player with a 40-50% market share. Beyond traditional advertisement portals, real estate agents can now resort to targeted social advertising. The new « Call To Action » Facebook service can offer a potential buyer visit dates at the same time he is visualizing pictures of the asset, whilst staying on the same Internet page. Snapchat or Instagram are two of the most used platforms by real estate agents to target future buyers. We can imagine also new systems that share information horizontally across the market, not only between agents, but with other participants in the transaction such as mortgagors, surveyors or even private individuals. Specific portals also apply to offices or retail premises.

Everyone now has access to the assets available on the residential market as well as on the commercial market.

Unlike other transactions in everyday life, a real estate transaction is characterized by a strong information asymmetry between the seller who knows the asset well, and the buyer who must make a decision in less than an hour, which will impact his life for decades. On savage metropolitan markets, there is little room for fact-finding and would-be New-Yorkers, Londoners or Parisians have to decide instantly if they take the apartment or walk away. Until now, a buyer knew almost nothing about the assets he coveted, from the quality of the technical facilities to the solar exposure throughout the year, or the level of pollution in the area. Various diagnoses required by regulations (real surface, quality of the electrical installation, energy consumption, presence of lead, termites...) during the transaction are an interesting basis, but they are far from perfect. The abundance of unknown data remaining is hurting the good functioning of the market. New stakeholders try to rectify this. Tomorrow, each building could have a true digital health booklet, allowing the one-click visualization of work history and energy consumption. The American startup HomeZada offers its clients the ability to enumerate the features of their house (type of construction, materials, heating, roofing, insulation, etc.). The digital document thus created will be forwarded to the future buyers of the house, bringing a welcome transparency. Another innovation: it is possible to know the soalr exposure of a property over a day or a year. Thanks to the French application Solen, users can measure the natural luminosity of an asset from a few pictures taken at the windows. An independent certificate is generated and enables users to check the sun exposure room by room, at any time during the year. The Solen algorithm notably takes into account the orientation of the asset, the glazed surface, the distance and whether the asset is overlooked. Better knowledge of an asset also comes from a reliable analysis of its direct environment. There again, many applications give the buyers information, by producing street by street data, ranging from pollution to the amount of convenience stores, and the crime rate. However, this influx of information is not always easy to understand for the buyer. In other words, he does not necessarily know very well what neighborhood best fits his lifestyle. This is why companies like Fypio have developed algorithms which provide advice to buyers regarding location. The latter, a Canadian startup created in 2013, give a questionnaire to the buyer and helps them define their preferences. It was bought in 2015 by OpenHouse, an American company in the same niche.

We can observe the value of apartment databases with all these features, including the associated plans. This data exists, fire regulations often require simplified maps of buildings, but they are not very consolidated. Several companies are working on the digitization of paper plans. MapWize is an example. A company now sells this data. This company is the manufacturer of automated hoovers

Roomba, whose machines delimit the space in order to know where to clean.

Once all these features are known, a price has to be set. This task, which used to be the prerogative of real estate agents, was widely automated by the creation of databases. The company CoStar, created in the 1980s, is the leader in office properties Big Data. The data from 4.5 million commercial real estate properties (offices, shops, logistics, etc.) is compiled, then sold to professionals who wish to better understand their market. CoStar is present globally, and had US$ 1 billion turnover in 2016, notably by relying on Apartments.com, a company specialized in residential housing data. It bought the company in 2014 for US$ 500 million. After years of having a monopoly, CoStar must now face competitors such as CompStak, Xceligent or RealMassive, which also flourish in the same niche. Even in residential housing, startups offer dynamic approaches. This is the case for HouseCanary, a Californian company which predicts the value of an apartment for the next three years by cross-referencing millions of socio-economic data. By comparing previsions with the actual transaction prices observed, the self-learning algorithms improve everyday. The ambition of Jeremy Sicklick, HouseCanary director, is clear: "We want to do for residential real estate what Bloomberg did for financial services – build a platform that will be a beacon of accuracy and transparency, enabling greater speed and confidence in residential real estate transactions." Since the fixed price may need to change according to demand, Triplemint is another startup able to give the right price daily, according to expressions of interest.

Finally, more and more companies are positioning themselves like platforms, coordinating the action of different stakeholders in the transaction, allowing for example the consolidation of all required due diligence, or the automation of the contract production. The French startup MyNotary speeds up the creation of the file because it is based on a collaborative logic between multiple stakeholders that are seller, purchaser, surveyor, diagnostician, trustee, banker, insurer, etc. Everyone can easily connect to the platform and provide the documents requested. In addition, a compromise of sale is automatically generated based on the information contained in the documents. This compromise can then be signed online by the stakeholders.

New distribution platforms on the buyers side are appearing, competing with intermediaries, riding on increasing criticism of intermediaries for their lack of transparency and their cost: between 5 percent and 6 percent in the U.S. and Canada, 3 to 4% in France, 2% in the UK.[25] Founded in 2004, Real Matters is a two-sided platform that aggregates more than 100,000 experts in the real estate sector. Individuals and businesses can find real estate agents, brokers in finance, or insurance brokers.

---

[25]Office of Fair Trading

Service providers are rated by customers after each performance. With this competition, the latter are less greedy and offer more transparency on their billing methods. The customer can choose the right service provider at the right price, without having to do a thorough search. Real Matters was introduced to the Toronto Stock Exchange in May 2017 in order to accelerate its development, after having raised over US$ 100 million in 2016. Real Matters already benefits from a market share of 16 % in this country. Many websites have an agent directory, and work like search engines. Depending on the criteria given (geography, tariffs, experience, etc), several agents are suggested to the client. In addition, agents are assessed continuously and their statistics are analyzed. This follow-up enables a better matching between client and agent, but also encourages the latter to fulfill his mission properly. Indeed, since the agent knows there is little chance of him also helping the client in his next acquisition, he may be tempted to offer a low quality service. The French startup Yanport offers sellers the ability to give a simple sale mandates to three different agents. Thus, during the entire sale period, each realtor can follow the activity of the other two trying to sell the same asset, especially regarding the price level. This transparency of information enables each of the agents to adjust their strategy on a daily basis. More generally, transaction professionals will survive if they consider sellers and buyers like customers, and not like users. As such, the sales strategy of French promoter Roxim can inspire others. Since March 2017, presales have a "satisfied or your money back" offer. There are many conditions to fulfill in order to get money back, but this sales technique illustrates this change of perspective perfectly. In the sales of new apartments also, the company HabX which raised US$ 12 million has considerably improved client experience by offering them the ability to co-conceive their future apartment, and even their future building. This renewed customer experience has had a very positive effect on the ability to market new dwellings.

In the end, the intermediaries still have a key role due to the ability to generate sales mandates, either by their access to privileged information during a testament or a divorce, or by their ability to convince undecided buyers to sell their asset by doing some fieldwork. However, this situation is threatened in two ways. On the one hand, word of mouth has increased tenfold with the Internet, and many sites reward the provision of qualified leads. They create looser networks of professional and non-professional real estate agents, able to source leads amongst their families, their friends, and their neighborhood. On the other hand, the predictive algorithms allow users to figure out who is likely to want to move and sell their property. Beyond the profiling of Internet giants, Google and Facebook being at the forefront, other companies have arrived in the same niche. The American company Smartzip provides a solution to aid in the management of accounts receivable

(CRM). The application can identify the 20% of people most likely to move in a particular district. This prediction is made by an algorithm and is based on multiple data sources: change of market prices, average duration average of occupancy of a dwelling, household profile, etc.

As it is easier to quickly generate revenues, the first entrants initially positioned themselves in addition to the key players, namely the intermediaries. Indeed, the share of sales between private individuals was very weak in the U.S. If many Americans first attempt to sell their property themselves, 89% of transactions are eventually completed with the help of a real estate agent. [26] And the figure is raising. In 1997, 77% of consumers worked with a real estate broker. Today a new generation of players is looming, by positioning itself as direct competitors of traditional intermediaries. They are direct competitors as they are mainly talking to sellers rather than buyers. These platforms are based on the division of the chain of operations, offering the customer the choice of which services he needs. Demand for the unbundling of services has resulted in the emergence of entities offering a reduced commission in return for the home owner performing some of the selling activities. For instance, platforms offer fixed pricing, so not proportional to the amount of the

---

[26]National Association of Realtors, 2015

transaction. In big metropoles, sellers increasingly refuse to accept the real estate agent service costing twice as much as ten years ago due to the increase in prices, when the service provision remains the same. In London, the startup PurpleBricks invoices a fixed fee of 1,300 dollars for London, and 1,100 dollars outside London regardless of the amount of the transaction. The company is responsible for the creation of the sale advertisement, as well as its publication on the Internet. The clients are let in charge of picking up the potential buyers and organizing home showing themselves. This company founded in 2010 is now worth US$ 1.6 billion. Other players like British Yopa, American Reali or Swedish Marton have adopted the same strategy. Last year, the Seattle-based Redfin has filed for a public offering with a public market capitalization of up to US$ 1.1 billion. Redfin combines an online model, in which consumers can browse homes and take virtual tours, and an offline model, in which real-estate agents whom the company employs meet with the home shoppers. It has a lower overall commission rate of 1% to 1.5% rather than the traditional 2.5% to 3%. Houzeo offers individual sellers a 100% digital assistance on the duration of the operation: estimate of the value of the property, online presence on all relevant platforms, recovery of administrative documents, comparison of bids and final act of sale. Thanks to the optimization of each of these steps, Houzeo drastically reduced delays. For example, the administrative authorities can access the platform to sign the document digitally. Also, they can follow in real-time the status of their case (processed, being processed or treated) with the notary or lawyer. Moreover, the company connects sellers with providers of services to further facilitate the sale. This applies to photographers or specialized assessors who are necessary for some transactions.

The American OpenDoor is also on the front line to replace traditional agents with a revisited intermediary role focused on transaction speed. Instead of finding a buyer for your asset, OpenDoor buys it backs directly, and then deals with the resale. The seller therefore transfers the two risks inherent in a transaction to the intermediary: the sale amount and the duration of the sale which is an average of 103 days in the U.S. [27] After raising new funds in November 2016, the newcomer is priced at US$ 1.1 billion. The disintermediation will go further as OpenDoor fits all its assets with a connected lock, in order to facilitate visits from potential buyers. The British Nested is a competitor of OpenDoor. In this case, the platform pays the seller 97% of the value of his property from the start then the residue after the actual sale. This type of model seduces the investors, as shown by the funds raised by Nested, US$ 43 million in October 2017. Two of the co-founders of Trulia raised US$ 33 million to launch Knock, which is intended to help sellers to sell their real estate in less than six weeks, for the same six percent fee that users would pay a traditional real estate agent. The company's

---

[27]Ryan Lawler, *OpenDoor gets another US$ 20 million to simplify the process of selling your home,* Techcrunch, February 26, 2015

home pricing algorithm relies on neighborhood analysis and a proprietary 200-point on-site inspection. Other startups help individuals to organize the auction sale of their apartment or house. Once reserved for exceptional properties, this type of sale is becoming democratized.

For traditional intermediaries, blockchain is also a serious threat. This new technology enables the decentralized storage of information with a high level of transparency and security. Another particularity: the recourse to a trusted third party intermediary is not compulsory with blockchain. Nicknamed « the trust machine » by The Economist, this technology can be likened to a large forgery-proof accounting register, which everyone can check. However, in the real estate sector, trusted human third parties are ubiquitous. This is the case for estate agents who play this role between buyer and seller. One way blockchain-enabled smart contracts could reduce the costs of transactions. Money and assets would be automatically transferred once conditions in the encoded contracts are met. Another way blockchain can give access to ownership of asset by dividing into multiple tokens. Deloitte Netherlands, Cambridge Innovation Center (CIC) and the city of Rotterdam are working on a first blockchain-based real estate app for recording lease deals on the distributed ledger. In 2016, the real estate platform Ubiquity achieved the first property title transfer via blockchain technology. The transfer was performed by

Marina Reznik, head of the real estate Department at Atlantic Sotheby's International Reality. In September 2017, the Californian startup Propy made headlines by signing a partnership with the Government of Ukraine. In fact, since January 1, 2018, foreigners can acquire property in Ukraine, and Propy offers to pay for these properties in crypto-currency. Michael Arrington, founder of TechCrunch, is committed to be the first buyer on the Propy platform. The company raised US$ 15 million in initial coin offering. At the same time, blockchain makes possible a multi-signature system. It enables all parties to work remotely without losses in reliability.

In addition to securing transactions, blockchain can also be used as land registry records. Several countries have already made this choice, such as Ghana, where the startup Bitland saves the titles of properties on blockchain. Until then, only 10% of rural land was listed in an official document. For others, the lack of address still causes enormous logistical problems. Other countries like Georgia are thinking about blockchain solutions to build their cadaster. Resorting to an incorruptible registry is a means to avoid land disputes, especially in countries where the rule of law is fragile.

And what about Bitcoin in real estate? Fewer than fifty buyers accepting bitcoin have listed homes on Realtor.com.

The transmission of property between parents and children could also experience mutation. The ageing of the population, coupled with the decline in pension insurance, encourages seniors to find other sources of income. In addition, the latter wish to stay in their homes as long as possible. In this context, everything suggests that life annuity sale will grow. This is evidenced by the success of the American Reverse Mortgage Funding startup. It has completely redesigned the user experience, by providing more transparency and monitoring to a type of contract that remains sometimes difficult to consider. The startup created in 2013 acquired more than US$ 200 million in 2014, and currently has more than 400 employees. The division of property is also a relevant answer to the problems of the elderly. The company Monetivia launched in October 2016 a new product allowing the investor to acquire the bare ownership, for about 60% of the market value of the property, while the seller keeps the usufruct for a defined period in advance, which can go up to 20 years. If the seller lives beyond this period and wishes to stay in their property, Monetivia, which recently partnered with Allianz, pays an annuity to the investor until the death of the person. The modeling of life expectancies by insurers enables very accurate estimates of the amounts to be paid. This initiative can help to get out of the traditional pattern of inheritance by the transmission of real estate, which makes less sense today in developed countries. Indeed, lengthening life expectancy delays the transmission against the children's own lifecycle. The latter inherit at 50 or 60 years old a residence their parents occupied in a suboptimal way for years, and for which they have no utility. Finally, certain existing business practices in other areas, such as rental with purchase option, are arriving in the real estate sector. This method of acquisition is a solution for buyers without a contract for an indefinite period - which means they cannot have a bank loan, but who still have a sufficient income to pay rent and save. It is notably the case of the self-employed, whose number continues to grow. Rental with purchase option is also a way out for sellers in less strained areas where demand is low.

Easing the rental management burden

Rental management therefore has good days ahead. This management is difficult because the interests of the landlord and the tenant are rarely aligned. First the tenant wants to be mobile, where the landlord prefers stability. The terms of the lease are the first stumbling block. Then the owner addresses issues of maintenance over the long term, while the tenant has a precise date, meaning the end of the lease, hence the problems around the inventory of fixtures. Finally, the landlord bears the risk of the insolvency of the tenant, and seeks ways to prevent it. In rental management as in the transaction, two types of solutions have successively appeared: modern SAAS software intended for property managers to improve the quality of the service provided, and tools for the individuals to dispense with traditional rental managers, often greedy in fees.

As for transactions, many landlord-tenant portals emerged during the late 1990s, by digitizing former paper advertisements. However, the services of these platforms have not changed much since their launch, and their market share stagnates. Today, a second generation of startups is starting in this trade. Among the new players, many two-sided platforms offer new services to improve matching. In the manner of dating sites, it serves to connect a landlord and tenant, taking into account the preferences of each party. This mission is beneficial insofar as these preferences are not always revealed in traditional ads. It is not uncommon that a tenant applies for an apartment when his file has no chance of being selected. To apply anyway is costly in time and money, which is harmful to the fluidity of the residential rental market. The process would be more effective if the selection criteria were more transparent. A major innovation is to indicate the probability that his candidacy will be selected. The estimate is made by comparing the expectations of the landlord against the quality of the file. In order to achieve this connection, the creditworthiness of the tenant and their guarantors is not the only criterion. The duration of the lease or the interest of the two parties also come into account. Other more usual services are also offered to landlords, such as making appointments online or scanning the inventory of fixtures. This revolution is also to the benefit of tenants, or rather of future tenants who benefit from an improvement in the quality of service, avoiding spending their time in aborted visits, having their personal data in contained in paper files and wasting their money due to sometimes failing intermediation services. Today, especially in metropolitan areas where demand exceeds supply, tenants are often badly treated and suffer from a relatively low quality of service. By allowing the best match between supply and demand, these tools will improve their first report to the estate, since a majority of these current tenants will also one day become owner.

There are also new tools available only to landlords. This is the case of the startup Rentify in the U.S. that uses new technologies to facilitate the rental of an asset. Big data for example enables landlords to accelerate and refine the process of valuation, and to avoid displaying too high a rent, which would not attract the tenant, or too low a rent, which would cause a shortfall. U.S Rentberry streamlines the entire long-term rental process using blockchain and smart contracts technology and eliminates the need for a middleman. The legal aspects are also affected by this revolution. In the U.S., the free software offered by startup Cozy enables the user to manage their property by automating the creation of rent receipts. Faced with the increase in regulatory constraints that govern the real estate market, how can landlords ensure that rental agreements respect the law? The French startup LeBonBail offers a service to landlords to reduce this uncertainty, which seriously affects the fluidity of the rental market by creating mistrust between the parties. It has developed a contract generating tool which meets the latest standards. The startup goes further than the simple automatic generation of contract: the platform enables the electronic signature of the contract. The whole procedure can happen online and be simplified, dynamic and fast. It is even possible to generate and sign the contract in about 10 minutes. Finally, the continuous update of the contract is offered. One could also imagine a service of regular visits by remote data transmission, in order to check that the housing is well maintained by the tenant, and avoid surprises at the end of the lease. These digital services allow individual landlords who do not live near the property they wish to rent to manage their property remotely with ease. It therefore promotes the acquisition of geographically more distant properties, allowing the extension of the market. A good example of simplified process is car parks rental. Several companies like WeSmartPark, ParqEx, SPOT or JustPark provide mobile applications that manage rentals, reservations, payment and a universal remote connected to access parking in lots of condominiums.

Finally, the owners are increasingly tempted to look for a return, leaving intermediaries to solve payment incidents. Leasehold insurances are riding high. In major cities the approval threshold is so high that people aren't able to get an apartment they could otherwise afford. Most landlords have crazy requirements such as annual income in excess of 40 times one month's rent. New York startup The Guarantors ensures coverage of unpaid rents for the landlord by issuing a surety bond, after having carefully selected the tenants through an algorithm. The service costs anywhere between 5-10% of annual rent but it avoids tenants having to put up a large security deposit or prepay months in advance. In China, Ziroom works with Ant Financial and Tencent on a social credit scoring, which enables the landlord to decide whether a person can rent such or such apartment.

The impact of these technologies on rental management modes, of which today 40 to 50% is directly made from individual to individual, is difficult to estimate. On the one hand these tools can make it easier for individual owners who reclaim their property. On the other hand specialized stakeholders realize extremely high economies of scale either from the point of view of the minimization of the vacancy or optimization of the equipment. In the U.S., after the real estate market collapsed in 1989, institutional capital flooded the market, aggregating large pools of apartment stock from the Resolution Trust Corporation Prior. They bring a more professional apartment properties management as well as new services to tenants. Today for large residential portfolio managers, the use of full software solutions also generates returns to scale, leading to a higher concentration. Vonovia is Germany's leading nationwide residential real estate company with a US$ 37 billion portfolio. Vonovia uses a SAP-CRM to manage around 355,000 residential units in all of Germany's attractive cities and regions. Just 1 per cent of the France and UK's private rented housing stocks are currently owned by institutions, compared with 13 per cent in the U.S., 17 per cent in Germany, 23 per cent in Switzerland and 37 per cent in the Netherlands, according to IPD, a data provider. These figures depend a lot on fiscal and public policies.

China is an extremely interesting case because the authorities have decided to encourage massive residential leasing as a way to counteract the rising prices. Today 190 million people rent across the country, this figure being expected to rise sharply in the upcoming years. This has prompted the biggest Chinese developers to announce plans to build millions of rental housing units, but also intermediaries to offer rental services. The startup Ziroom, a spin-off of the transaction giant Lianja, launched in 2016, already manages several hundreds of thousands of lots through nine Chinese cities, and hopes to reach 1 million by late 2018. It mainly manages lots from individual owners which are brought up to standard, and for which it provides standard furniture. Visits for interested tenants happen without a human agent. Everything is done simply through the application, which unlocks a connected lock. Ziroom rents the apartments at a price higher than the compensation requested by the particular landlord, and pockets the difference. The total collection for 2017 amounted to US$ 2.4 billion. To finance its development, the company raised US$ 630 million with Warburg Pincus, Sequoia and Tencent in January 2017.

Real estate is not so much efficient. Even in the most expensive cities there is a high percentage of vacant space. Short-term rental platforms U.S. Airbnb, Indian Oyo or Chinese Tujia and Xiaozhu highlighted an offer previously unexpressed in apartments or houses empty for a short period. Note that the distinctions between the one and the others eventually blur: Expedia or Booking now rent housing from individuals, while Airbnb has announced it references boutique hotels on its platform. However, this rental mode involves substantial logistics. That's why many concierge services are launched in complementarity with the aforementioned platforms. Hostmaker is the first platform of networking in Europe between independent concierges and landlords. This website enables owners to delegate the management of their apartments with a package of *à la carte* benefits provided by concierges, from welcoming travelers to the inventory at the time of departure, as well as linen cleaning. These are evaluated after each performance. Atlanta-based Rented.com covers six continents. It has launched a US$ 125 million fund to guarantee rental property income and turnkey management service to homeowners. After accumulating enough data, these platforms may also report to the owners the right time to rent their property based on demand, or when they can make a profit from sleeping elsewhere while renting their property for more money. In the end these startups no longer sell services so much as a financial investment with a return. Some data platforms compiling the revenue, occupancy & pricing of properties help you to gro your vacation rental business. AirDNA combine over 5,000,000 properties rented. One can also imagine a fully automated renting process. After signing a "smart contract" through blockchain, the selected tenant receives an activation code that will open the electronic lock of the apartment he wishes to occupy for a more or less long period. A digital observation is conducted and compares the status of the apartment with the digital model established at the departure of the previous tenant. Once the occupant is gone, an automatic message will be sent to a cleaning company so that the apartment is ready for another rental. It is no coincidence that Airbnb bought ChangeCoin in 2016, a startup specializing in micropayments using decentralized network technology at the origin of the bitcoin. Bee Token is a decentralized Airbnb project, based in the San Francisco Bay Area, offering tokenized short-term rentals, without a middleman. So far, the company has raised roughly US$ 10 million. Another way to reduce vacancy rate, it is to accept subletting. Flip is a housing platform legally facilitating subletting an apartment for a long-term stay, giving renters greater flexibility and landlords greater security.

Following Airbnb, many stakeholders started to facilitate short-term rental of specific parts of the home, from the kitchen (The Kitchen Network, The Food Corridor) to the basement (Spacer, ex-Rooster). Note, however, that many of these business models occupy a grey area from the point of view of the regulator. Because they divert the whole property from its original aim, or sometimes happen without the approval of the owner (sublease), they have prompted bans both in condominium buildings regulations and in local legislations. The latter often demand a record of properties on Airbnb and set a maximum of nights that can be offered for rent.

Short-term rentals are of interest to asset managers. Vornado real estate fund has created the WhyHotel startup to rent apartments in a building newly delivered for very short durations, until they are assigned to traditional long-term tenants. In London, Lowe Guardians converts empty buildings into clean, safe and cheap housing. It creates an affordable pop-up structure that can go inside a larger space to create a private bedroom. For building owners hoping to turning them into modern housing, having temporary residents provides free security and sometimes offer a tax break. Rent are about 50% below market prices.

Rental management in commercial real estate is also changing. A cultural revolution distinguishing property and occupation already happened in this segment of the market. There was a time where businesses were proud to own the walls of their offices or factories, as were hotel operators. Starting in the 1990s, this preference for ownership was gradually weakened on the business side. The U.S. were the first to take this turn. At the end of the 1990s, two-thirds of office buildings in the U.S. were occupied by renters, not owners. This real estate divestment is such that in 2004, a quarter of the 40 largest French market cap stocks had no more real estate management.[28]

There are now, as with residential, two-sided platforms where landlords and owners meet. StoreFront for example, is a London startup that connects owners of retail space and potential takers. In office property, players like Truss completely rethink how to rent space. While paper is still very widely used by traditional brokers, this company has created a 100% digital process for future tenants of office space. In addition to the traditional multi-criteria search engine, applicants have access to the plans in 3D of all available assets. This service is made possible by a partnership with the company Matterport. It is also possible to make an appointment online for a physical visit. Finally, a chatbot is accessible and answers prospective tenants' questions. This virtual assistant enables considerable time saving and a reduction in rental costs. There is even an Airbnb of warehouses called Stowga, which has signed a strategic partnership with CBRE in December 2017. Meeting rooms are also affected. Breather, a Canadian provider of on-demand meeting rooms and workspaces, has raised about US$ 40 million in a Series C financing, bringing its total funding so far to nearly US$ 73 million.

At the same time, new tools are made available for large business owners to help them manage their portfolio. The

---

[28]Observatoire du Management Immobilier, Essec, 2005.

champion of the sector is unquestionably VTS, an American company that has raised over US$ 100 million since its creation in 2011. Thanks to this tool, the owners can track real-time performance of their rental portfolio: contact information of the occupants, compile a list of leases, and view statistics on vacancy rates, etc. The communication between landlord and tenant is also directly via the platform. VTS also uses big data to advise donors on trade-offs within their portfolio. For example, it may be advisable for the owner to opt out of a city where the trend is negative, in order to reinvest in a more promising region. This platform enables the user to see the different stakeholders on a building. Finally, marketing documents are automatically generated whenever a property is vacant and therefore needs rebooking. These assets may even be promoted directly to end customers. VTS merged with Hightower in November 2016, another provider of solutions for the commercial real estate portfolio managers. The new group is estimated at a value of US$ 300 million. VTS now has more than 6 billion square feet (550 million sqm) of space on its platform. These tools are much more effective especially since they benefit from the increase in scale resulting from the merger. More data allows refinement of the forecasts on the platform. It is no coincidence that Blackstone, the biggest asset investment fund manager of the real estate world with US$ 110 billion under management, participated in the first fundraising of VTS. On the other side of the world, Equiem's platform has been adopted by

10 of the 11 largest Australian property owners representing 44 million square feet (4.1 million sqm) of premium office. The software help landlords to better connect with occupants and enhance customer experience.

Finally, advances of semantic analysis will have a major impact on rental management. The German startup Leverton is specialized in the extraction of data contained in a lease: start, end, amount of rent, conditions for extension, etc. This work, currently done by hand, is tedious and lengthens the audits, which ultimately slows the execution of a transaction.

The evolving role of asset manager

Like in the residential sector, these innovations are questioning many habits of the sector. The preference for a single tenant in the building is no more. Indeed, the cost of managing an additional taker tends to be zero thanks to new digital tools. Also, an office building with multiple tenants is a less risky asset. The price of the asset is an increasing function of the number of tenants who occupy it.

The innovations also lead to reclaiming the management of the property by its owner. The role of asset manager or REIT, is evolving, the number of intermediaries decrease and logics of integration are at work. This handling of operational management has long existed for buildings where users are just passing by. Managers of shopping centers are specialized and manage their assets themselves, improving occupation, seeking to increase customer satisfaction by investing in technologies and tools. The hospitality sector has also followed this path. Since 2005, major hotel chains began to embark on a policy of outsourcing, selling their walls to concentrate their financial resources on managing and promoting their brand. The trend is being reversed: building owners will no longer be at the mercy of a hotel operator who could decide to sell, and they no longer hesitate do business themselves. The business of hotel operator is based on two skills: customer acquisition and operational management of the business. Since the emergence of gigantic market places like Booking.com or Hotels.com, traditional hotel operators have more control of the marketing they offer. To become a hotel, the owner must learn to assemble cleaning and catering teams in addition to the traditional management of the building. This is what Starwood has done for many years by directly operating hotels, and directly seeking financing from investors via Starwood Capital. The group now manages nearly US$ 30 billion. The strategy of Foncière des Régions, with US$ 24 billion in assets under management, is fully invested in this new trend. Traditionally confined to its role of owner, financiers favor since 2014 a combined formula of acquiring premises and business assets. The group thus bought and manages hotels. The same thing happens today with offices, and it will happen tomorrow in the residential sector. To embrace the coworking and coliving revolutions, some private equity funds has invested in operators: Blackstone in The Office Group, Brookfield in Convene, Gaw Capital in Naked Hub and Brockton Capital in Fora.

To get the value of an asset, even a core one, you need to get your hands dirty. Shorter leases need to be managed, new services offered to users, data collected and analyzed. To do so, having access to the data is necessary, and a passive investor delegating the management of its assets cannot do this. It is not a niche success, addressing a specific customer, but rather a global phenomenon of platforms that make a promise in productivity and in square feet. And this promise is scalable, justifying their value of several billion dollars. The arrival of Vision Fund in WeWork in summer 2017 happened with a valuation estimated at US$ 19 billion, just seven years after its creation. Besides this, such know-how can also be sold. Thus now WeWork provides design, construction and management services to large corporates asking for WeWork to customize their space than lease one of its shared offices. In 2015, WeWork bought Case, a 60 persons BIM-consulting firm to design and build out its tenant spaces, with the goal of improving replicability. WeWork's second acquisition was Welkio, a digital sign-in system for guests at an office. In 2017, WeWork bought FieldLens, a mobile application that aims to digitize traditional communication between building owners, contractors, subcontractors and architects on a construction or renovation project. The company raised US$ 8 million in Series A funding in 2014. Latest

WeWork acquisition was the digital marketing and advertising company Conductor. Gradually, year by year, WeWork improve its tool kit to become a fully-integrated provider of office space. In the end, these platforms have the upper hand over fund managers who currently crave for interesting projects. They can even do without, like WeWork did, by launching WeWork Property Advisors, their own property company in association with private-equity firm Rhone Group. As Dror Poleg, the founder of Rethinking Real Estate, points out *"Rhone [could] benefit from the increase in value of the actual buildings that WeWork operates—a bit like McDonald's' realization that its buildings are more valuable than its burger business or that both are worth owning."*

On the residential sector, there is the Airbnb initiative, which began to move up the value chain with a partnership around a new, branded 324-unit apartment complex in Kissimmee, Florida. Apartments will be designed to meet short-term rental requirements, keyless doors and secure storage. The partner for the so-called "Niido Powered by Airbnb" is the Miami-based developer Newgard Development Group. The tenants in this building will be explicitly allowed to short-rent their apartments for up to 180 days a year. Each property could ask for help with cleaning and check-in through a special application.

Moving to predictive maintenance

Buy, sell, rent and maintain, these are the missions of a property owner. These missions are not daily, but every decision can have major consequences. The profitability of a real estate asset brings an influx - rents - to a stock - invested capital to acquire the property. This equation assumes that the value of a real estate asset is fixed in time. However, real estate is an asset like any other, the value of which tends to decrease over time due to wear and tear, with a limit price related to the property sector. Containing the wear and tear of an asset has a direct impact on its profitability, all the more since regulations requiring an upgrade of buildings, offices like houses or hotels, are multiplying. This objective is reached through a more effective maintenance, taking advantage of the historical knowledge of the building. However, the sector of the real estate maintenance long remained closed to innovation. The RICS, professional body institute, which seeks to standardize the standards in this sector, points out that the profession of facility manager has always been considered a secondary profession. [29] In the absence of productivity gains, and therefore of the ability to reduce the full cost, the cost pressure often resulted in a decline in construction cost and a report on the current charges. Too costly, maintenance is sometimes delayed. It can result in extreme cases like these condominiums so degraded that repair works eventually offset the value of the housing unit

---

[29]Rapport de l'institut RICS, 2017.

owned. Today, the practices are evolving and innovation resumes its rightful place.

The individual owners, whether they occupy the property or rent it, must work to rejuvenate their asset, or repair a damage to a technical element after that it appears. Either they take care of this work themselves, or they call upon a craftsman. In the first case, platforms such as ManoMano which raised US$ 74 million in 2017 gives them access to a huge catalogue of tools and materials previously reserved for professionals. The owner can view tutorials on YouTube in order to acquire new skills. However, resorting to professionals is quickly needed. Unfortunately, the asymmetry of information between an individual and a craftsman on the nature of the malfunction leads to prohibitive prices, particularly in emergency locksmith or plumbing repairs. New platforms provide the necessary price transparency of the services and make an assessment of the craftsmen possible. Guests of these platforms only have to send a photo of the work to do, and they receive a fixed price offer in the following hours. A large part of the activity of these platforms comes from apartment renovation work. These platforms improve transparency and adjustment between supply and demand in a market of development and renovation work estimated at more than US$ 800 billion in the U.S. and Europe, and where the quality is often lacking. In France, only half of individuals having to make energy improvements to their homes had been satisfied. [30] Amazon launched as early as 2015 Amazon Home Services, offering to help U.S. individuals to find a craftsman to carry out work at home. When purchasing material on the e-commerce site, a button offers to find a provider to install it. To be part of the list, professionals are duly selected and must give a part of their profits. The work is also verified by the online auction site. Another giant, IAC, merged in June 2017 HomeAdvisor and Angie's List, two platforms linking work providers and individuals. The new platform will see 17 billion services provided annually by more than 200,000 different providers. IAC also has the platforms 123devis.com and Travaux.com in France, MyHammer in Germany, MyBuilder in the UK, HomeStars in Canada, each having a large position in their respective markets. Startups like Houzz thrive on this niche. This company goes beyond its role of intermediary between owner and artisan and offers advice to individuals in need. For the professional, Houzz is a simplification tool likely to generate productivity gains. The platform facilitates the usual steps of the provider (whether it be a visit before work, quotes, invoicing, payments, subsidies and help available, as well as administrative certificates) and the professional can thus focus on the essential. Tolteck is a software designed for craftsmen to improve the management of quotes and invoices, manage their calendar, and their portfolio of

---

[30]Observatoire Permanent de l'amélioration Energétique du logement, Campagne 2015. *Travaux achevés en 2014, janvier 2016.*

clients. The platform, which was acquired by French construction materials giant Saint-Gobain in December 2017 is also intended to supply building materials and tools for these craftsmen. Other platforms, Taskrabbit being the most famous one, connect homeowners and renters with vetted non-licensed professionals who can perform a variety of home improvement works.

Professional asset managers also improve their corrective maintenance. In residential buildings, the corrective maintenance sometimes includes common facilities and therefore it is the responsibility of the joint-property manager. Until today, information travelled poorly between the owners, the trustee and the providers, where the repair time is often an issue when the heating breaks down, when a pipeline explodes or when a window is broken. Digital technology makes possible shorter delays between the problem and its resolution. This is done through a better identification of malfunctions. Several companies for example sell sophisticated tools for insurance claims by occupants to the traditional co-ownership property manager. With a picture of the disaster, the competent provider is automatically contacted and can intervene as soon as possible. IoT gradually substitute the human in the reporting. First, they replaced humans in the surveys of consumption with smart meters, and now in the detection of problems. For example, a valve equipped with a sensor can detect a water leak on a pipe, even if the leak is hidden from view. Such products are proposed by Meetflo or Buoy. The smart water metering market is expected to reach a size of US$ 5.5bn by 2021.

Other companies study the deformation of buildings such as Morphosense, French startup. It installs sensors on superstructures (bridges, dams, etc.) and then networks them to measure geometric deformation of the structure in 3D and the way it vibrates, and operates maintenance before the occurrence of problems. Contextual data such as weather or temperature are added. The precision is 9 microns per feet. Tomorrow these solutions might come to buildings. Drones are also used to detect technical problems, particularly for the maintenance of the facade and roof. The Dronotec company relies on drones to make the inspection of buildings safer, faster and less costly. A more upstream identification reduces the cost of repair, providing that the intervention of the technician is quick. In this intervention niche can be found one of a few unicorns of the Real Estech: Sms Assist. This American company connects property managers with external providers they need. Everything goes through the cloud, from pictures taken by the repair before and after the intervention to the invoices. Here again, the evaluation system causes a natural selection that increases the average level of service.

Because most of the damage is covered by buildings insurance, the interface between insurers and operators of maintenance must be improved so that there are no cash advance fees. For the owner, the challenge is also to find insurance that covers all of these risks but which does not overlap with other previously subscribed insurance. Several companies now allow the owner to digitize all these insurance contracts in order to identify duplicates. For the insurer, the presence of sensors helps prevent damage. This is why Generali Switzerland encourages clients to adopt accessories connected to the house. In collaboration with the retailer Media Markt, the insurer offers a discount on connected devices, which have a preventive character (cameras monitoring, motion, smoke, or water detectors). The discount is offered to individuals subscribing to a full household insurance. California-based insurtech company Hippo has secured US$ 25 million in Series B funding, led by Fifth Wall. The company goal is to reinvent homeowners' insurance by using big data collected in municipal building records, satellite images and smart home devices. In emerging countries, microinsurance is an indispensable tool for the development of real estate markets. The MicroEnsure company provides this type of product in several African countries. This startup that has raised US$ 10 million in 2014 currently has 40 million customers, 85 percent of which had no insurance before.

Finally, the intervention will be more effective as the digital model of buildings will be widespread. This model will help the repairman to make the right choices in telling the history of the building, and repairs already made. BIM will be even more useful where several trades simultaneously conduct maintenance work. Better communication will reduce the risk of error. To do so, updating regularly the BIM model and sharing its access is necessary. Another revolution to anticipate in the maintenance sector are the 3D printers. A number of pieces are rare due to the age of the building and the technical systems, or because their sellers are in a situation of oligopolies. They are sold at high prices and can take a long time to be received. Scanning and 3D printing of parts to be changed could be a decisive parade, the limit remaining for now, as in the automobile sector, insurance. The move from after-sales service technicians, employed by large groups, towards independent professionals, like the startup WeMaintain enables, is also an interesting path to bring down the prices of these services.

Predictive maintenance, also called preventive maintenance or analytics, is the next step. Thanks to the abundance of data generated daily by a building, it is possible to predict coming malfunctions. At least two consequences are immediately obvious. On the one hand, replacing a facility before it falls down leads to a reduction of maintenance costs. On the other hand, a relatively detailed predictive analysis provides an ex-ante maintenance cost of a building. Tomorrow, investors will be able to predict the amount of maintenance expenses to anticipate for the years to come. The elevators are a very substantial part of buildings budget. As a consequence, ThyssenKrupp Elevator partnered with Microsoft to develop predictive maintenance software package. Startup companies are positioning themselves on this niche. This is the case of Uptime, that already predicts 80% of breakdowns of elevators through its sensors. Autodesk, the BIM software company, partnered with Nutonian, a company specialized in machine learning. Together, they will be able to go even further in the analysis of the data of the IoT and progress on preventive maintenance.

CHAPTER 4 -
MAKING THE USER A PRIORITY AGAIN

In 1951, Heidegger gave a conference entitled "Building, Dwelling, Thinking" in Darmstadt. Heidegger argues that in the modern times we have confused in the understanding of relations between building and dwelling. Building is too much more conceived as a functional need in providing shelter or housing. Building as dwelling is a part of a community and enables this community to experience a mutual sense of the present. Building as a dwelling is also to spare, to preserve the earth. At the time, such thoughts were secondary to the rebuilding effort. And yet it is the very meaning of real estate. Even the future of the smartest building ever constructed is ultimately all about the people inside.

The occupation of real estate (housing, office or warehouse), like mall attendance, depends on their attractiveness. This attractiveness is the relationship between the services offered and their cost. However, the services expected by the users have varied considerably in recent years. Household and business life has evolved. Apartment-share, that are not always suffered but desired, as well as stepfamilies with children from different relationships, require more flexible spaces based on departures and arrivals within the dwelling unit. Economic activity is increasingly spasmodic and volatile. Companies are more mobile, subjected to increasing competition with stronger requirements for adaptation. The space they occupy must be able to evolve more frequently and more quickly. In this modern economy, workers occupy a greater number of jobs during their careers and tend to move more often, and so to change housing. IKEA offers low cost products adapted to the multiple new steps in the life of households. Its success shows how the cycles have accelerated.

It is obvious that the first factor of attractiveness is the location. Competition for the best assets has not declined, on the contrary it has increased. The concentration of talent necessary for the activity of services with high added value results in the increasing attractiveness of the most central metropolitan areas. Enrico Moretti perfectly described this phenomenon in his reference book, *The New Geography of Jobs*.[31] Some places have always been more successful than others, but these differences have increased rapidly over the past three decades. The growth is concentrated in a handful of cities. Simply put, three reasons explain these effects of concentration. The first is the depth of the labor market. If you are in a highly specialized position, you want to be on a labor market where there are many employers looking for workers and many workers looking for employers. The same logic applies for intermediary service providers. For example, companies based in Silicon Valley will find these services in the form of lawyers specializing in intellectual property,

---

[31] Enrico Moretti, The New Geography of Jobs, Mariner Books, 2013.

laboratories, incubators and investment funds. And because they are so specialized, these providers are particularly good at what they do. The third factor is what economists call the impact of human capital: the fact that people learn from their colleagues, random encounters in a café, at the kids' school. People tend to exchange information, employment opportunities, information technology, or a collaboration proposal. The founders of very high growth companies have rarely met in a virtual meeting.

In the cities, low quality real estate assets can still find takers because of their central location. However, even in these privileged environments, the strong rotation of real estate assets means maintaining a high level of attractiveness, and thus a permanent improvement. Even homeowners are concerned because they may need to change place more often, and so have interest to maintain a high level of attractiveness of their premises if they sell them or rent them later. A problem appears when the services offered are not valued by the occupant. The interest of the owner and of the occupier may seem opposites, the first can be tempted to reduce the benefits available to display a discount, and leave the occupant with loads of associated costs.

A limited consumption

Since the needs of the occupants have evolved, they do not simply obey a strategy of minimizing the costs of rent, but are studying all the charges associated with the occupation of a property. The time where the owner did not care about energy performance, because he could recover the energy and water costs in rental charges, is gone. The era when in condominiums, consumables were shared by the whole building is also gone. Requests for individualization of consumption are increasing. In numerous countries, regulation made mandatory the energy performance diagnostics. During the construction, performance benchmarks can be requested like BRE Environmental Assessment Method (BREEAM) in the UK, Leadership in Energy and Environmental Design (LEED) in North America, Green Star in Australia or Haute qualité environnementale (HQE) in France – they are becoming widespread.

Experts estimate that the renovation of buildings could reduce consumption of energy for heating, cooling, ventilation, and hot water by 60 to 90%. Currently, the annual rate of renovation in the European Union is 1%. If it increased to 3%, consumption could be reduced by three-fourths by 2050. Nearly half of the consumption of a building is devoted to heating, ventilation and air conditioning. This area was a focal point of innovation. In addition to innovations in material - purification by ultraviolet or photochemical reactions - a large number of startups work to improve energy management in existing buildings. Deepki offers a solution that turns existing data especially from bills into action plans for energy efficiency using algorithms. The job is to collect all the existing data and cross them with external data in order to establish an energy profile for the building without adding any new costly sensors. FirstFuel developed a technology allowing users to calculate potential energy savings by using massive amounts of data. In the U.S., a company like Kinetic Buildings, using self-learning algorithms can determine the less efficient HVAC systems in a building and promises savings in the range of 20 to 30%. Livable Analytics, on the other hand, founded on the campus of the University of California at Berkeley, has built a platform for building managers to know their occupants' satisfaction in relation to energy savings. Canadian Distech Controls provides unique building management technologies and services that optimize energy efficiency. Blackstone invested in Entic, technology company that optimizes energy usage in large buildings, to roll out the solution throughout its buildings portfolio. What is happening at the level of the building is also valid at the level of the apartment or house. Google acquired Nest for US$ 3.2 billion in 2015, a smart-thermostat manufacturer. This thermostat learns from users' habits: it lowers the heating in the absence of the occupants and detects the time needed to heat or cool the home in order to use the minimum energy. Sense raised US$ 14 million in 2017 with its super-accurate energy disaggregation device, building on work in the speech recognition field. Thermondo became the largest installer of heating solution in Germany applying digital process. The company completed a US$ 21 million financing round last year.

The savings associated with the lighting of buildings is known, notably due to the replacement of traditional light bulbs with LEDs and OLEDS low power consumption and long lifetimes. The generalization of LiFi as method of transmitting data at speeds sometimes superior to Wifi, should continue to push for the renewal of the fleet of light bulbs. Enlighted, an American company has developed sensors to reduce electricity consumption up to 70% without losing light. Windows equipped with sensors can measure the brightness and interact with bulbs to ensure optimal consumption. These solutions, sensors, Internet of Things and software, are sometimes gathered under the names « smart building » and « smart home ». They designate a building that is more resource efficient and easier to live in.

Finally, the last area of improvement of energy efficiency is related to the insulation of buildings. Some companies try to imagine more modern solutions to indoor and outdoor insulation by using phase change materials, for example. Tom Lipinski, founder of Q - Bot, has tried to answer the challenge of soil insulation, which is very costly and tends to not be effective for a long time as a result of movements of land or the building. He has developed a robot equipped with a 3D scanner and a foam gun that projects a layer of insulation under the floating floor, reducing the loss of heat by 85%. The company was created as a result of the Retrofit contest for the Future, an initiative launched by the British agency for innovation with the ambition to upgrade 100 houses across the country with the objective of reducing CO_2 emissions by 80%. Finally, the use of the roof space is a field still full of promises, be it for the production of electricity but also for agricultural production activities. All that is left to question is the installation of solar panels with a limited sustainability and imported with a very negative carbon balance. The use of the only indicator measured with reliability - the effects of greenhouse gas emissions - seems more relevant.

Building As A Service

Like the owner, the occupant now researches a package of services, so he can avoid spending time finding those services by himself for the duration of the lease. These services can include maintenance providers, cleaning, air conditioning, home, heating, maintenance of safety standards, taxes, insurance, and management of the furniture. We do not buy square feet anymore but a complete service. This is the first reason for the success of shared workspaces in which managers charge for a single service that integrates all of these. In concentrating and pooling shared workspaces, these solutions can realize substantial savings. The company Regus, created in 1989, became the biggest flexible offices solutions provider with 2,300 offices. More than 14,000 shared offices are spread over the globe against less than 1,000 a decade ago. Since then, co-working spaces have flourished globally, offering ever more services for occupants, from a bar to yoga classes. In recent years, China has experienced a surge in coworking spaces. UrWork, a Chinese co-working space firm founded by a real-estate veteran, already claims nearly 90 locations in 22 cities in China, Singapore, London and New York, housing 40,000 people. It is backed by Sequoia Capital and has been valued at US$ 1.4 billion. UrWork announced its merger with its rival on the domestic market, New Space. Local rivals include Naked Hub and KrSpace.

This model happens more and more in housing. All of the benefits available to the tenant are centralized in a single bill including access to a gym, a swimming pool, a nursery. The apartments are fully equipped, they are cleaned, laundry and household products provided. Landlords offer to provide furniture, as do Fizzy Living in London in exchange of a 8% surplus on the rent for three years. Chinese landlord Ziroom provides the same furniture in all the apartments it rents on behalf of individual owners. Here, there is still a separation between ownership and use. Today, few people pass on their furniture, which was so common a generation ago. In the end, a consolidated service is not far from a hotel service.

The more services are individualized and numerous, the more users are changing rapidly, the more they must be able to restrict access to some parts of the building. This explains the dramatic growth of the global market for connected locks, which will be worth US$ 24 billion by 2024 according to GrandView Research. For the user, the connected lock offers a flawless experience, either by concentrating multiple keys in a single object, in general a smartphone, either by biometric recognition. In offices, this electronic key enables access to the coffee machine, as much as access to the building, or to book a meeting room. In the residential sector, equipment rates are 60% in South Korea or Japan, and already of 4% in China. The U.S. are progressing very quickly. Only Europe is lagging behind this movement. US-based smart lock maker August Home was bought by Swedish lock giant Assa Abloy. August Home's revenues for 2018 are expected to be US$ 60 million. These locks have accompanied the development of short-term rental. In residences with services, they make it possible to know who has access to the pool or the gym. They open remotely when the owner is away to let the cleaning staff or delivery person in. Amazon launched its security camera plus connected lock bundle, which allows its delivery drivers to deposit packages into customers' homes and even turn apartment into buildings' package hubs. In recent months, the online retail giant acquired wireless home-security camera maker Blink for an undisclosed sum and video doorbells maker Ring in a US$ 1 billion deal. Ring had 2 million customers and sales of US$ 160 million in 2016.

The building as a service also makes it possible to better know the behavior of customers. With this, it becomes possible to offer custom services or content. This requires an accumulation of data. The smart home offers a unique opportunity to collect data thanks to its remotely controlled appliances interacting together. Many startups offer smart devices, but a 2012 Nascent Object study showed that 80% of smart devices for buildings used only 28 basic electronic components. Their multiplication is a source of waste, notably due to a lack of standards. A centralizing platform for this data is the issue. Ziroom TV, switches and thermostats are connected to the company's application, which all tenants have to download. Operators are increasingly trying to convince their customers to use their applications. In recent months, the success of connected speakers such as Amazon Echo or Google Home, powered by personal assistants Alexa and Google Assistant, sold respectively 31 and 14 million units in the U.S. This enables the conception of a possible standardization around a single user interface. This market will represent US$ 122 billion in 2022 against 45 in 2015. Recently, Amazon decided not to sell any of the newer products from Google's smart home division Nest, heating up the war over the future of the smart home. The competition will be driven by the aging of the population, as these devices can foster home support.

In offices, customer behaviors are studied through movement sensors, cameras, smart devices, in order to know what environment is more conducive to work. Thus, WeWork is able to measure the level of attention of an audience in a meeting room. Anthony Slumbers, Estates Gazette columnist, considers that AI in the commercial real estate industry will make asset manager able to understand exactly how everyone who uses buildings, spaces and places really does use them.

Malls were the first to invest in these technologies. Hundreds of millions of dollars have been invested by CBRE, Unibail, Simon Property Group and Westfield to follow the customer experience inside the building, measure customer attention when they look at displays and shelves, and create loyalty programs including targeted coupons. Unacast, a location data startup from Norway, closed a US$ 17.5 million Series B round led by White Star Capital. Unacast getting tons of human movement and behavior data from hundreds of data supplier partners pulling on GPS signals from cell phones. Unacast's clients use it for all sorts of purposes from targeted marketing to real estate and retail planning. Location data is more and more complex to interpret and clients require not just data, but the context to extract value from it. But some experiments resulted in costly experiments for disappointing results. Let's remember the failure of the beacon, these micro-transmitters affecting phones of a dedicated application, and which were to revolutionize retail. Since consumers are less likely to download new apps, this invention could hardly survive.

Then, this services package must be sized according to the needs of the tenant. From the point of view of the professional tenant, particularly in the case of offices, the transformation of a lease into a service contract makes it more flexible. It frees the tenant from minimum periods, born by the taker. This makes it possible to imagine leaving a place within one month. Conversely, it is possible to ask for more space to accommodate an extra activity. The site manager is responsible for the balance between supply and demand. This approach greatly increases the mobility of the tenant who can either extend a site or decide to move. Its managers generally have several offices in the same city, and sometimes have access to sites in other cities. Then all they need to move are their paper archives, when previously moving would involve transporting large amounts of furniture. Even large companies begin to use these solutions in addition to their own housing stock, to caps demand peaks. For the biggest real estate owners, having a direct relationship with the final customer enables them to accompany the customer throughout their entire lifetime value. This is especially true in the office market, where a young startup can go from a few offices to several thousand square feet, before becoming a real company with a whole building. This can also be valid in the residential market, where the owner must be able to accompany a young single person when they start having kids, and even help them become owners later.

The mobility of users leads to the modularity of the building itself. Kasita, a startup in Austin, produced standardized living spaces that can be assembled with each other and even moved. Inside, mobile partitions allow to customization and improvement of the living space. Google is aware that the needs of its organization will evolve in the coming years. It plans to produce its new North Bayshore in Mountain View campus with modular capabilities, as evidenced by the models revealed by Heatherwick and Bjarke Ingels showing glass tents animated by cranes. Modularity is also required for housing, in order to adapt to changes in the size of families. In France, the Group SNI, manager of 200,000 social housing units, has developed a floor prototype made of mixed wood and large-span concrete, which enables the creation of 40 feet (12 meters) wide spaces, free of any post. In addition, the backbone consists of solid wood beams, in which layers are inserted for water, air, energy and communication networks. Without posts, and with a bathroom and a kitchen that can be repositioned at will, the building is very flexible.

Building As A Community

The constitution of the community building (Building as a Community) is the transformation of what was once experienced as a constraint into a competitive advantage. When the crowd becomes a community. This is what makes the difference between a co-working space and the likes of WeWork, Common or Starcity. They are not selling square footage anymore, but productivity powered by the crowd. WeWork thus measured the optimal distance of a corridor so that people can cross without being embarrassed and start talking. The constitution of a community of companies working in the same space also offers the chance for people to meet. A study covering 2,000 workers, led by Dylan Minor, Professor at the Kellogg School of Management, and Jason Corsello, senior Vice President at Cornerstone OnDemand, showed that the best way to increase productivity is to sit by an employee with a high productivity. Replacing an employee with an average productivity by an employee who is twice as productive leads to a contagion effect among the surrounding workers, and increases their productivity by 10% approximately.

In 2017, North American offices will average 151 square feet per worker (14 sqm), according to real estate data provider CoreNet Global. That's down from 176 square feet (16 sqm) in 2012 and 225 square feet (21 sqm) in 2010. Employers used to put more workers in less space to reduce office costs, now pushing employees closer together is a way to encourage interaction and increase productivity. In a world where innovation happens by serendipity, meetings can take place spontaneously between specialists of different disciplines, and between employees from different companies. The arrival on the labor market of new workers will accelerate the trend. Millennials state they are 82% be more productive when they work in a co-working space.[32] They are also 86% more likely to consider co-working as enabling them to

---

[32] Coworking by the Numbers, GCUC/Emergent Research, 2015

increase the size of their professional network. Marie Schneegans created NeverEatAlone so that occupants of a same building take the time to meet during their lunch break. Over 50 companies subscribed to this service. Now called WorkWell, the application gathers all services offered to the occupants of a building on a same interface, becoming a professional social network. The asset manager themselves offers this service to the occupants to improve the building's attractiveness. Content must be generated to feed the community. This is the reason why WeWork acquired a stake in Cheddar media to broadcast the videos produced by the startup in its co-working spaces, instead of traditional channels of information which deemed too impersonal and not in resonance with the concerns of active young people. Workers in Tishman Speyer's New-York buildings, are able to download the Zo app that let them book amenities like a haircut or a yoga class. The app will eventually spread to its entire global portfolio, illustrating how fierce is the battle between rival landlords to rein corporate tenants by appealing to their employees. Workplace Edge is a similar app designed by Cushman & Wakefield.

Co-working inspired co-living. Everybody knows apartment-sharing popularized by Friends sitcom but most importantly which is all most young people can afford. And the experience can be a nightmare. Acasa is an app helping the world's growing population of young renters to live better together by set-up, manage, split and pay your bills. U.S Bedly is platform trying to improve the classic Craigslist search by offering already furnished apartments and a US$ 100 monthly fee which includes utilities, WiFi, twice-a-month cleaning. Co-living push things one step further. Community in a residential building means access to more shared services. Residences with services were very expensive to their occupants, even when sharing costs with other tenants. Space must be shared more in order to reduce costs, thus making them more accessible. In other words private spaces are slightly smaller in order to increase common areas built to foster interaction. This can be done with similar people that have shared interests. It's the principle of apartment-sharing on a larger scale. Companies like WeLive, Ollie or Common have the ambition to produce such buildings. WeLive has created more than 400 co-living apartments in New York and outside Washington, D.C., and recently announced a third project in Seattle. They wish to offer studios as well as shared spaces like a lounge, a kitchen, a rooftop, a gym, a laundry and a co-working space. Coliving is spreading very quickly. It is not only for a handful of young adults. The co-living microflats market now accounts for 5-10% of Britain's US$ 35 billion build-to-rent private rental sector, according to James Mannix, head of residential capital markets at property group Knight Frank. The biggest co-living building in the world, The Collective Old Oak containing 550 bedrooms, was actually built there. Traditional players operators with big ambitions are entering into the coliving market. Property Markets Group for instance plans 3,500 units in the next five years, built and operated by a new branch of the company called PMGx. Israeli Mindspace has experienced a meteoric growth. In China, Mofang Gongyu raised US$ 300 million in April 2016 to expand its renting activity to apartments in complexes offering many shared services aimed at young urban professionals. Coming Space, based in Nanjing, has just raised a US$ 20 million fund to finance its international expansion, aiming for the UK, Japan and Singapore. Above all, these buildings host a community, which needs to be animated around shared passions. This is the main benefit of these places. You+, supported by the founder of Xiaomi, transforms old industrial buildings into co-living spaces with kitchens, offices, a gym and shared cinemas. The company already manages 100,000 lots of 320-540 square feet (30-50 sqm) around the country. The monthly rent varies between US$ 250 and 475. Above all, the tenants are all connected on the application where they can participate in themed nights, do sports together or gather around their passion for photography or music. OneThird opened its first building in Madrid and employs a full-time community manager to animate the space.

If this version is the ultimate extent of co-living, there are also less ambitious steps. New platforms are trying to enrich the communication inside the building to facilitate the loan of infrequently used objects between individuals, or dedicated events. The notion of community also means people trust each other to carry out maintenance tasks collectively. Co-tenants can deal with minor repairs themselves, maintain green spaces and clean public areas, which reduces expenses. The unicorn Nextdoor organizes this notion of community across the neighborhood. The private social network already has a dozen million users registered on in the U.S., the UK, the Netherlands, and has just expanded to France.

Building As A Hub

A frozen community does nothing. For a community to be rich, it must be open, dynamic and attractive. The building must become a full-fledged hub to constantly increase its attractiveness. Office buildings are being gifted with strong architectural moves, graphic prints, a name, even with a press agency or through presence on social networks. Observation decks are even conceived in the biggest ones, such as the Shanghai Tower or 30 Hudson Yards in New York. Thousands of tourists come to visit them like they would visit an attraction. The quality of the connection to communication networks is key. It is WiredScore's mission, a New York company that has been working since 2013 on building certification based on the quality of their fiber optic connection and coverage of mobile networks. Today, more than 1,000 buildings in more than 80 cities are already certified.

Shopping malls have always been hubs, but this attractiveness imperative has significantly increased with the emergence of e-commerce. In the U.S., where the retail area per capita has always been much higher than the rest of the world (24 square feet against 16 in Canada, 11 in Australia, 4 in the UK), the situation is even more critical and many shops are closing. It has been described as a retail apocalypse. Foot traffic continues to slow in the 1,100 or so indoor malls through the U.S. as customers abandon succumb to e-commerce. All managers of shopping centers are engaged in researching new services capable of attracting customers. Some malls are trying to reach targeted audiences by choosing sometimes equivocal names, others play on loyalty and emphasize the privileged nature of the members. A movement of convergence between retail activities and leisure activities even gave birth to the word retailnment, the intersection of retail and entertainment. Concerts, performances, film screenings are organized. This requires a minimum size to make up for these extra expenses. Thus the French Unibail, which recently bought the European and American activities of Westfield, is relinquishing malls that had less than 10 million annual visitors. Other managers have abandoned the idea of being places of destination, to become places of flow and enjoy the effect of natural passage in railway stations or airports. At the same time, a merge occurred between physical spaces and online sales sites. Physical and digital fusion gave birth to the concept of multichannel. Sales are taking place on the Internet but the act of purchasing happens in a showroom, and the reception of the package is done in-store. All physical corporate brands develop or support an online sales channel. The reverse movement is also emerging: Internet giants are developing physical distribution locations. Amazon thus set up temporary shops in its name in Germany. Amazon bought out the existing network of supermarkets of organic products Whole Foods for US$ 13.7 billion in June 2017. They are now testing supermarkets without checkouts where you can pay by facial recognition and connection to smartphones. Sometimes however, the expected returns of multichannel never happen. Macerich, one of the biggest malls managers in the U.S., spent US$ 10 million in the Waltersupply startup. The goal was to help European sellers to expand their presence overseas through ephemeral stores with screens and sensors. However, the deployment of their solution proved to be much more complicated than expected.

A quality animation has become indispensable for office managers. In a not so distant future, winning workplaces will be those able to attract a crowd. The power ratio will be turned upside down, between event organizers who today pay to rent spaces, and the people who own those spaces. There might even come a time where the organizer of quality events, allowing the meeting of ideas or the animation of a co-working location, will be paid by the owner of the premises. WeWork acquired an interest in MeetUp, an event handler. This is part of a strategy to have events on all the time. They will sometimes be held by third parties to the building, but will ensure mingling and a renewal of the community. Tenant demanding to be paid to occupy your space seems crazy? It already happens in retail and starting in office when a tenant brand is so powerful that it can attract other tenants.

A place cannot rely on a short time window to become iconic - the day for offices, the weekend for trade, and the night for residential. The building becomes a multi-purpose space mixing housing with offices, shops included at the beginning of the planning, but also public facilities. This also wards off any drops in activity related to mono specialization, which is what is happening with retail today. Accor, the world's fifth largest hotel group, decided to create a permanent flow in its hotels, which goes beyond the guests coming to stay there. The trend has long existed when it comes to restaurants or bars. Nowadays, offers have extended to fitness centers. Through the recent acquisition of Nextdoor, an important co-working operator in France with nearly 330,000 square feet (31,000 sqm), Accor wants to include offices in its hotels. WeWork is not only focused on office space but the "We" brand includes co-living spaces like WeLive, wellness facility Rise by We and an early childhood education program WeGrow. The company also acquired the coding bootcamp Flatiron School. In this perspective, the so-called retail apocalypse offers huge opportunities. Million square feet of perfectly located struggling retail space would be converted in residential or office space. In December 2017, mall operator GGP rejected a US$ 14.8 billion buyout offer from Brookfield Property Partners. The Canadian asset manager could have leveraged its expertise in office development to restructure shopping centers facing retail bankruptcies and store closures. Just to mention some emblematic revamps in recent months. In Beijing, the Cofco Plaza has been transformed from a shopping center to a 390,000 square feet (36,000 sqm) co-working space. The revamp has meant that the office area is already generating four times as much rental income as it did when it was a furniture retail space. In Los Angeles, owner Macerich and Hudson Pacific Properties will redevelop the Westside Pavillion mall, keeping 100,000 square feet (9,200 sqm) of retail while turning 500,000 square feet (46,000 sqm) into offices. In New-York, the Canadian retailer Hudson's Bay Company (HBC) sold its iconic 676,000 square feet (62,800 sqm) Lord & Taylor building on Manhattan's 5th Avenue to WeWork Property Advisors.

CONCLUSION

These thoughts on the real estate of the future are not purely prophetic. Rather, they are anchored in concrete examples, considering companies that open new paths onto which customers will rush. Time in real estate terms is long on many aspects. However, the industry can also follow the new mantras of platforms, growing returns, and hyper-growth. This is not a time for the timid. The dynamics of the most innovative companies is accelerating. They increasingly have the means to afford their ambitions. Globally, the number of startups rose from 176 in 2008 to 1,274 by 2017. In the same period, cumulative investments in these startups soared from US$ 2.4 billion to US$ 33.7 billion.

These companies are increasingly brought to light during major events such as the smart home at the CES in Las Vegas. Reed-Midem, the organizer of the great real estate MIPIM show, dedicated two exhibitions, in Paris and New York, to promote Real Estech. Traditional networks of real estate experts climb on the bandwagon. The Urban Land institute has arranged a Proptech conference in Berlin. Today, 17 companies operating in the real estate sector are regarded as unicorns, in other words private companies whose theoretical value exceeds US$ 1 billion. Among them 10 are American (Airbnb, WeWork Katerra, Houzz, OpenDoor, SMS Assist, Procore, NextDoor, Compass, Ten-x) and 6 are Chinese (Lianjia, Mofang, Fangdd, Aiwujiwu, Xiaozhu and URWork). Among them, two decacorns, Airbnb and WeWork are valued respectively at US$ 23 and US$ 19 billion. Both are also involved in the proliferation of the sector by investing huge money.

Tomorrow, there will be even more unicorns. Real estate has long been an asset of diversification for the tech entrepreneurs. The Sawmer brothers, founders of the famous Rocket Berlin Internet incubator, invested in a traditional real estate fund in New York, Avente Capital. Now these talented entrepreneurs want to change the sector. Experienced professionals who have successfully completed one or two endeavors are getting adventurous, bringing new skills in an area formerly shunned by talent. The founder of Katerra served as interim CEO of Tesla in 2007. Sector funds have emerged, allowing fundraising to grow even more. Among them are Fifth Wall (US$ 232 million), Navitas, RealTech, Moderne, Camber Creek, Sansiri, Corigin, MetaProp, Traverse, C31, Brick & Mortar, PiLabs, BlackPrint. Once cautious due to the slow pace of return on invested capital, renowned VC are no more reluctant to invest. Andreesen Horowitz bet on Airbnb, Frame, Zumper, Point; Greylock Partners bet on Redfin, Airbnb, Matterport, Zumber NextDoor. For Thrive Capital it is Compass, Cadre, Opendoor, Hightower, Honest Buildings. Felicis Ventures chose OpenDoor, Floored, Matterport. Very dynamic communities exist around DisruptCRE, Concrete, Asia Proptech. For now, continental Europe is behind in this movement. 55% of Real Estech fundraising happens in the U.S., 25% in Asia, 9% in the UK. France and

Germany share the remaining crumbs. New York is the real epicenter of this movement with almost 10% of the fundraising. Global real estate services firm JLL estimates that 179 proptech startups in Asia Pacific have raised US$ 4.8 billion since 2013.

There are some established players of real estate among the subscribers of these funds. Other large groups are investing directly, such as Blackstone, Silverstein, Brookfield Property Partners, Rudin Management Company or SL Green Realty Corp. They recognize these real estate business models will inevitably be the convergence between traditional assets and technology. The example of Invitation Homes is illustrative. Blackstone has created this dedicated entity in 2011 to buy foreclosed houses. The value created is a mix of hard and soft value adding notably vendor management tools, budget tracking and inspection software, customized workflow, online payment system. In 2017, Blackstone listed Invitation Homes on the NYSE which later merged with Starwood Waypoint Homes, creating the largest single-family rental platform in the world. The company is now worth around US$ 11 billion. Real estate increasingly attracts technology giants, Google, Apple, Facebook, Amazon, Microsoft, Baidu, Alibaba, Tencent, which see it as an important market for monetizing their knowledge of customers. Superfunds like Vision Fund created by Masayoshi Son are also very interested in the real estate topic. Vision invest in three Real Estech last year: Compass, Katerra and WeWork. They are joining

Oyo and Mapbox including mapping solutions which can also be used inside buildings.

At the macroeconomic level, this revolution will have significant impacts. Currently, almost all of the inputs of real estate, from materials to financing, from workers to maintenance, are generally less than 30 miles (50 kilometers) away. Tomorrow, with digitization on one side and prefabrication of construction on the other, this added value will become mobile. Let's consider the impact on tax and employment! We live at a time where technology will enable the transformation of the local real estate industry into mobile industry. All these stakeholders and their employees should ask themselves how to react faced with this "evaporation" of part of their added value. In the hospitality industry, with booking platforms, a significant part of the value of the night has already been relocated with strong consequences, including from the tax point of view. The digitization of the sector has two impacts. On the one hand value becomes mobile, and is no longer directly related to the proximity of the property. On the other hand value is concentrated in the hands of the biggest stakeholders, who generate economies of scale. If this phenomenon does not happen immediately because the real estate cycle is still long - around ten years when electronic goods have a six times faster rotation - it has already started. In this context, remaining passive and believing customers will always prefer to deal with someone with an office close-by is not enough.

This wave of innovation can only take form with a favorable regulation. The real estate sector is seen as unproductive by nature, due to its overwhelming inability to generate productivity gains. Some politicians and economists no longer hesitate to make it a target of choice, imposing a tax hell. Yet, far from a fantasized club of people of independent means living off rents, entrepreneurs, innovators, and trailblazers are coming back to the real estate sector. This second revolution is still in its infancy and requires substantial investment from all stakeholders. Unnecessarily aggressive taxes on the final product of the market would soon nip in the bud all attempts to innovate.

The options for change we suggest in this book are valid in the current technological framework of mobility and communication. Regarding communication, the strong assumption of this book is that people want to meet, see each other, touch, and feel each other in real life. There are countless prophets announcing the end of cities, saying communications technologies will allow everyone to telecommute and live in a decentralized manner. It is understood that "everyone" often means service workers with a strong added value. The case of Automattic, Wordpress editing company, is known. They closed their 15,000 square feet (1,400 sqm) headquarters in the heart of San Francisco where Uber, Twitter and Airbnb coexist. Only five people out of 30 employees came to the office on a daily basis, others preferred to work remotely. The company boasts about recruiting via Skype and offering new employees a 2,000 dollars bonus to organize their home office, as well as 250 dollars a month to get to co-working spaces. However it would be a mistake to consider this atypical case common. In 2013, Marissa Mayer, President of Yahoo had limited telecommuting to force teams to work side by side and stimulate creativity. In February 2017, IBM also decided to slash work-from-home policy, adopted by 40 percent of its employees, in order to improve its productivity. Similarly, theories predicted the death of air transport for business reasons due to the advent of conference calls. Yet, millions of people still travel, sometimes over very long distances, to sign a contract, meet a partner, and encourage their teams. All of these being actions they could perform remotely. Pierre Nanterme, the CEO of consulting firm Accenture with 435,000 employees, already uses hologram technology to simultaneously talk to the executives in 200 different cities. It's possible the improvement of this technology will someday replace physical meetings. However, this seems far away, as it would question the social character of our species.

The consequences of technological changes in transportation seem, conversely, much more tangible. Let's imagine that the autonomous car becomes widespread tomorrow: hundreds of millions of square feet will be returned to the city, free to be built on. McKinsey calculated that by 2015, with the simple evolution of the car shape due to automation (no more pedal, steering wheel...) have the potential to reduce parking space by around 61 billion square feet (5,7 billion sqm) in the U.S. Let's imagine the Hyperloop becomes a reality tomorrow: it will change our relationship to distance. The Hyperloop consists of a double tube raised under low pressure to limit the friction of air, in which capsules carrying passengers or goods move. In theory, the Hyperloop, with a top speed of 760 mph (1,200 km/h), would connect San Francisco to Los Angeles in less than half an hour. That is a little faster than a plane, which currently travels this distance in 35 minutes. The revolution of real estate will then probably be different from what is stated here.

The evolution of real estate has already begun. When it becomes a revolution, it will move huge volumes, in terms of value, savings and jobs across the world. It will be eminently positive, freeing resources now tied up in obsolete production processes. It will be very positive, as it will respond to a need for improving the quality of buildings, adapting them to new uses. The smart cities of the future will be made of smart buildings, relying on intelligent networks of energy, communication, transport and waste.

AUTHORS

Robin Rivaton, robin.rivaton@realestech.eu

He worked at the Boston Consulting Group before serving as advisor to the CEO of Paris Airports Group. He is now CEO of a 100 persons agency in charge of attracting foreign investors in the Paris Region and very active in European tech.

He has been the economic advisor of Mr. Le Maire, current French Minister of Economy and Finance, and Mrs Pécresse, President of the Paris Region.

Lecturer in economics, he wrote 4 non-fiction books and maintains a regular media presence in various daily newspapers.

Vincent Pavanello, vincent.pavanello@realestech.eu

In charge of real estate investments in Europe for a single family-office, he is also an expert for a think-tank on economics and housing.

He led significant commercial real estate investments in Poland, Portugal and Romania.

Together, in 2016, they have created Real Estech, the first community for innovative stakeholders in real estate in France. www.realestech.eu

In June 2018, they will launch Real Estech Ventures, a US$60 million venture fund dedicated to European proptech startups.

The top 100 Real Estate startups (ranked by total fundraising)

#	Startup	Debut	Description	Fin. (M$)
1	WeWork (U.S.)	2011	WeWork provides shared workspaces, technology startup subculture communities, and services for entrepreneurs, freelancers, startups, small businesses and large enterprises	5500
2	Airbnb (U.S.)	2008	Airbnb is a community marketplace for people to list, discover and book spaces around the world through mobile phones or the internet.	3300
3	Katerra (U.S.)	2015	Katerra is an off-site construction company that is optimizing every aspect of development, design, and construction	1100
4	Lianja (China)	2001	Lianja (HomeLink) is an O2O (online-to-offline) real estate agency service provider.	926
5	Houzz (U.S.)	2009	Houzz is a platform for home remodeling and design, providing people with everything they need to improve their homes from start to finish	600
6	Mofang (China)	2010	Mofang Gongyu is one of the largest institutional rental apartment companies in China with projects across all tier one cities and select tier two cities across the country	500
7	OpenDoor (U.S.)	2014	Opendoor is an online homeselling service aimed at streamlining the sales process down to a few days.	320
8	Fangdd (China)	2011	FangDD is an online to offline (O2O) real estate platform that	305

#	Startup	Debut	Description	Fin. (M$)
			facilitates transactions between property sellers and home buyers through real estate brokers in China	
9	Iwjw (China)	2014	Iwjw or Aiwujiwu is a Shanghai-based online real estate agency	305
10	Xiaozhu (China)	2012	Xiaozhu.com is a Chinese booking website for daily rental and short-term rooms.	270
11	SMS Assist (U.S.)	1995	SMS Assist is a cloud-based multisite property management platform	255
12	PropertyGuru (Singapore)	2006	PropertyGuru.com is Singapore's largest property classifieds portal in terms of traffic	235
13	Procore (U.S.)	2002	Procore is a cloud-based construction management software application built for the construction industry professional, striving to make project management effortless, one task at a time.	229
14	Real Matters (Canada)	2005	Real Matters is a Canadian online platform that enables real estate agents to appraise property values, check on insurance inspections, search for titles and close mortgages.	227
15	NextDoor (U.S.)	2010	Nextdoor is a private social network that enables members to communicate with neighbors.	211
16	Compass (U.S.)	2012	Compass is a tech-driven real estate platform that puts technology at the fingertips of its agents and clients to streamline and transform the process of finding a home.	208

#	Startup	Debut	Description	Fin. (M$)
17	BluHomes (U.S.)	2008	BluHomes makes modern premium prefab homes that can be customized by Client through a 3-D Configurator (homes are built in half the time of traditional custom homes).	197
18	URWork (China)	2015	URWork is a Chinese co-working space operator	186
19	Onshape (U.S.)	2012	Onshape is a full-cloud 3D CAD system that lets everyone on a design team work together using any web browser, phone, or tablet.	169
20	Redfin (U.S.)	2005	Redfin provides real estate search and brokerage services through a combination of real estate web platforms and access to live agents.	167
21	LendingHome (U.S.)	2013	Lending Home is a technology-enabled marketplace that brings together borrowers and investors to improve the mortgage process.	166
22	Blend (U.S.)	2012	Blend's technology delivers speed and efficiency to lenders, so they can serve the modern borrower and safely navigate the industry's changing rules and regulations.	160
23	Ten-x (U.S.)	2007	Ten-x is an online real estate marketplace for residential and commercial real estate.	140
24	CADRE (U.S.)	2014	Cadre is an online marketplace that connects qualified investors and operators and provides a sophisticated technology product for managing processes	133

#	Startup	Debut	Description	Fin. (M$)
25	VTS (U.S.)	2011	VTS provide a leasing and asset management platform that empowers landlords and brokers to better attract, convert and retain their tenants.	111
26	ApartmentList (U.S.)	2011	Apartment List is a web and mobile based apartment rental marketplace for simple and delightful home-finding.	109
27	Placester (U.S.)	2008	Placester is an all-in-one business platform for real estate professionals with beautiful lead capturing websites, lead management, email marketing, marketing automation, analytics, free education and 24/7 support.	100
28	Zillow (U.S.)	2005	Zillow is an online real estate marketplace for finding properties.	87
29	Proptiger (India)	2011	Proptiger is a Indian digital marketplace that guides home buyers from the start of their home search to home loans and property registrations.	85
30	Nest Labs (U.S.)	2010	Nest Labs is a home automation producer of programmable, self-learning, sensor-driven, Wi-Fi-enabled thermostats, smoke detectors, and other security systems	80
31	Enlighted (U.S.)	2009	Enlighted is an IoT platform for commercial real estate that helps asset manager increase efficiency and make better decision	80

#	Startup	Debut	Description	Fin. (M$)
32	VivaReal (Brazil)	2009	VivaReal is an online real estate marketplace that connects buyers, sellers, and renters with properties in Brazil.	75
33	Manomano (France)	2013	Manomano is a platform for Home and DIY Lovers community that exchange tips and advice on their DIY or gardening project	73
34	Anjuke (China)	2007	Anjuke is an online real estate marketplace	72
35	OrderWithMe (U.S.)	2011	OrderwithMe is an on-demand retail platform for brands to quickly open turnkey omni-channel stores in major cities.	70
36	Breather (Canada)	2012	Breather is a Canadian app that provides an on-demand network of private, professional meeting rooms designed for work, meetings and to focus.	69
37	Roofstock (U.S.)	2015	Roofstock is an online marketplace that invests in leased single-family rental homes in a transparent, low-friction method.	65
38	HouseCanary (U.S.)	2014	HouseCanary is a source for accurate, uniform information that covers every residential block and property in the U.S., analyzed and visualized real-time to make better, faster decisions.	64
39	Common (U.S.)	2015	Common is a Colinving operator that offers private furnished bedrooms in beautiful shared suites, competitive rates, free	63

#	Startup	Debut	Description	Fin. (M$)
			utilities, weekly cleaning, and more.	
40	CommonFloor (India)	2007	CommonFloor enables users to buy, sell, and rent residential properties online in India.	63
41	Matterport (U.S.)	2010	Matterport is using computer vision and sensor technologies to provides end-to-end 3D virtual media solutions.	62
42	Realtyshares (U.S.)	2013	RealtyShares is a Crowdfunding platform which pools together debt and equity investments for apartments, office buildings and retail centers	60
43	PlanGrid (U.S.)	2011	PlanGrid is a construction productivity software that provides real-time updates and seamless file synchronization over Wi-Fi and cellular networks.	59
44	Yopa (UK)	2015	Yopa is an online estate agency that charges a fixed fees to sellers	58
45	Homelight (U.S.)	2012	HomeLight connects home owners looking to sell with real estate agents in their area who are likely to close quickly and get the best price for their homes	56
46	Prescient (U.S.)	2013	Prescient is a technology and manufacturing company that offers a faster, greener and more cost-effective alternative to conventional building structures.	53
47	Projectfrog (U.S.)	2006	Project Frog develops component buildings that assemble easily onsite for architects and builders to create energy-efficient buildings.	52

#	Startup	Debut	Description	Fin. (M$)
48	Bond Collective (U.S.)	2013	Bond Collective provides shared and luxury workspaces for modern businesses and individuals to be productive in a sophisticated environment.	50
49	Nested (UK)	2015	Nested is an online real estate agent that provides a cash advance to help sellers buy a new house before you've sold their old one	45
50	Better Mortgage (U.S.)	2014	Better is a direct lender dedicated to providing a fast, transparent, and online mortgage experience backed by superior customer support.	45
51	RealtyMogul (U.S.)	2012	RealtyMogul is an online marketplace for real estate investing, connecting borrowers and sponsors to individual and institutional investors.	45
52	Nestaway (India)	2015	NestAway is an Indian "Home Rental Network" attempting to provide better rental solutions via design and technology	43
53	Reonomy (U.S.)	2013	Reonomy is a technology platform that provides a simple and easy way for brokers, investors and lenders to sort through commercial real estate information and find deals.	40
54	Hippo (U.S.)	2015	Hippo offers intuitive and proactive home insurance by taking a tech-driven approach.	40
55	Lendinvest (UK)	2013	LendInvest is a marketplace platform for property lending and investing and a mortgage provider	39

#	Startup	Debut	Description	Fin. (M$)
56	HonestBuilding (U.S.)	2012	Honest Buildings is the an integrated, data-driven project management and procurement platform purpose-built for commercial real estate owners and managers	39
57	Knock (U.S.)	2015	Knock is an online home trade-in platform that uses data science to price homes accurately and technology to sell homes quickly	35
58	EquipmentShare (U.S.)	2014	EquipmentShare is a construction machinery marketplace that bring more efficiency to the buying, selling, and lending of equipment, which ranges from backhoes to bulldozers and bandsaws.	34
59	Habito (UK)	2015	Habito is an online mortgage broker that use a robot-adviser that helps people find and apply for the best deal	33
60	Fundrise (U.S.)	2011	Fundrise is a crowdfunding platform that allows a range of investors to fund commercial real estate projects.	33
61	Guest to Guest (France)	2011	GuestToGuest is a social network whose members exchange their homes during their vacation.	33
62	Zumper (U.S.)	2012	Zumper is a real-time home and apartment rental platform for tenants and landlords to find and rent apartments.	32
63	OfferPad (U.S.)	2015	OfferPad relies on technology to make offers to homeowners, who value the certainty of a sale and the ability to close within days over getting the highest price	30

#	Startup	Debut	Description	Fin. (M$)
64	SmartZip (U.S.)	2008	SmartZip offers innovative and effective predictive marketing solutions to help real estate agents get more listings and lenders more leads.	30
65	Zameen (Pakistan)	2006	Zameen is software that is specific to Pakistan in assisting individuals in navigating the real estate market.	29
66	Opcity (U.S.)	2015	Opcity connects real estate agents and mortgage loan officers to pre-screened, live leads.	27
67	LiquidSpace (U.S.)	2010	LiquidSpace is an online marketplace and workspace network for renting office space	26
68	NewForma (UK)	2005	Newforma provides mobile, cloud & desktop applications to enable owners, designers, builders and extended construction teams to collaborate.	25
69	Knotel (U.S.)	2015	Knotel provides customized headquarters for companies of 20 to 500 on flexible terms.	25
70	PatchofLand (U.S.)	2013	Patch of Land is a real estate marketplace lender that uses data to provide transparent, scalable, and efficient lending solutions.	25
71	McMakler (Germany)	2015	McMakler is a real estate agency, using a fixed pricing model and combining the traditional service with web-based technology.	25
72	Clara (U.S.)	2014	Clara is building technology to reduce the time and cost it takes to originate a mortgage and	24

#	Startup	Debut	Description	Fin. (M$)
			creating a more personalized, clear experience for our customers.	
73	Credi Fi (U.S.)	2014	With data on over 2.2 million properties and Commercial Real Estate loans, CrediFi's mission is to bring information transparency to this industry	23
74	Property Partner (UK)	2014	Property Partner combines residential real estate crowdfunding with a secondary exchange upon which investors can trade their holdings	22
75	Finalcad (France)	2011	Finalcad provides mobile apps and predictive analytics that help construction stakeholders anticipate and fix issues found during the building's journey.	22
76	Compstak (U.S.)	2011	CompStak employs a crowdsourced model to gather commercial real estate information for investors, brokers, asset managers and appraisers.	22
77	PropertyFinder (Dubai)	2015	Propertyfinder.ae is the largest real estate website in the UAE with a wide range of residential and commercial properties for sale and for rent.	22
78	Built (U.S.)	2014	Built is a provider of secure, cloud-based construction lending software that helps reduce construction loan risk, increases loan profitability, transforms the borrower experience, and simplifies compliance.	21

#	Startup	Debut	Description	Fin. (M$)
79	PeerStreet (U.S.)	2013	PeerStreet is a crowdfunding platform that gives investors easy access to high-yielding loans that are collateralized with real estate.	21
80	Appear Here (UK)	2013	Appear Here is a marketplace for short-term retail space.	21
81	BuildingIQ (U.S.)	2009	BuildingIQ is an energy management software platform, forecasts energy demand and adjusts buildings' HVAC settings to optimize energy use.	19
82	Meero (France)	2014	Meero provide photos, videos and virtual tours to sellers and real estate agents in less than 24 hours	19
83	Asset Avenue (U.S.)	2013	AssetAvenue is an online lender that is using technology to improve the way people borrow money for real estate investment properties	19
84	Cozy (U.S.)	2012	Cozy is a platform to streamline interactions between property managers and renters	18
85	Roomi (U.S.)	2013	Roomi is a peer-to-peer shared housing marketplace making it safer and easier to rent rooms and find roommates	17
86	OpenAgent (Australia)	2012	OpenAgent.com.au is a platform where sellers can compare and hire real estate agents	16
87	Exporo (Germany)	2014	Exporo is an Internet platform that offers investors the opportunity to invest in real estate projects through crowdinvesting	16

#	Startup	Debut	Description	Fin. (M$)
88	RealScout (U.S.)	2012	Through RealScout, home buyers can search for real estate using more personal criteria, such as "natural light," "high ceilings," "large backyards," and "gourmet kitchens."	16
89	Pillow (U.S.)	2014	Pillow Homes offers on-demand property management services for short-term rentals, such as via Airbnb	16
90	Leverton (Germany)	2012	Leverton develops and applies disruptive deep learning technologies to extract, structure and manage data from lease agreements	15
91	Propy (U.S.)	2016	Propy integrates blockchain ledger for the governments to make title deeds issuance for property instantly online, secure and cost-effective.	15
92	Mynd (U.S.)	2016	Mynd leverages technology, systems and data to more efficiently manage multi-family residential buildings with 50 units or less as well as single family rentals.	15
93	BuildZoom (U.S.)	2012	The company simplifies the process of selecting a general contractor and improving the outcomes of remodeling and construction projects. By gathering and analyzing information on 3.5 million licensed contractors and 100 million improvement projects	15
94	BrickVest (UK)	2014	BrickVest is an Online Real Estate Investment Platform that	14

#	Startup	Debut	Description	Fin. (M$)
			directly connects investors with a wide variety of real estate investment opportunities in a safe, easy and transparent way.	
95	Emoov (UK)	2010	eMoov is an online real estate agent that helps its clients with technology tools to sell their households	14
96	Spotahome (Spain)	2014	Spotahome is a rental site for mid to long-term accommodation in the world offering thousands of personally-checked properties with virtual viewings on the site that include photography, HD video tours, and floor plans.	14
97	Rentlytics (U.S.)	2012	Rentlytics is building the platform to transform the world's real estate data into accessible information to help real estate investment management firms	13
98	Amitree (U.S.)	2012	Amitree is an online platform that helps home buyers navigate the process of buying a house and agents build closer relationships with their clients and better anticipate their needs.	13
99	2nd Address (U.S.)	2014	2nd Address provides premium extended stays and corporate housing for business travelers.	12
100	Habx (France)	2016	HABX is a startup specializing in the configuration of new homes, via an innovative digital solution reversing the usual process of a classic real estate development operation	12

Source: Crunchbase, as of February 27, 2018

Our top 20 most promising Real Estate startups (founded after 2014)

#	Startup	Creation	Fin. (M$)	Description
1	Truss (U.S.)	2016	9	Truss provide a chatbot to help small and medium tenants (under 10,000 square feet) to find the right office spaces for them.
2	Workwell (France)	2016	2	Workwell is the office app that has a mission to make employees happier and more connected at work.
3	Trussle (UK)	2015	6	Trussle is a free online mortgage broker that uses Big Data analytics to find the best deal for its clients.
4	Houzeo (U.S.)	2017	-	Houzeo helps owners get maximum exposure to sell their home fast without real estate agent.
5	Envelope (U.S.)	2015	4	Envelope's 3D web app helps urban real estate industry professionals visualize and run scenarios on development potential under zoning.
6	Reali (U.S.)	2015	10	Reali is an online estate agency that charges fixed-fees to sellers.
7	Homie (U.S.)	2015	8	Homie is a peer-to-peer real estate marketplace where buyers, builders, and sellers of homes can meet without a middleman.
8	Acasa (UK)	2015	1	Acasa is an app helping the young renters to manage and share household expenses with multiple house members.
9	AirDNA (U.S.)	2015	-	AirDNA offers analytics tools that allow Airbnb and short-term rental managers and investors

				to optimize pricing and profit potential.
10	99.co (Singapore)	2014	10	99.co is a map-based property search engine that provides renters, buyers, and agents fast and efficient property search experience.
11	DroneBase (U.S.)	2014	7	DroneBase is a startup that connects drone users with individuals or real estate agent are interested in getting drone footage of a property.
12	Deepki	2014	3	With Deepki, use the data you already have to optimize the management of your property portfolio and engage in the Energy Transition.
13	Nestpick (Germany)	2014	10	Nestpick's platform is a tool for anyone to move anywhere at any time, connecting tenants and landlords around the world.
14	Flip (U.S.)	2015	3	Flip is a marketplace for flexible housing that make it easy to sublet, get out of a lease or find a flexible place to live.
15	Riley (U.S.)	2016	3	Real estate brokers buy leads and Riley Concierges text those leads basic questions within five minutes, qualify them, and pass them back to the realtor.
16	WeMaintain (France)	2017	2	WeMaintain is a B2B platform linking elevator skilled technicians and professional clients (office / residential trustees).

17	Viirt (U.S.)	2014	1	Viirt is an on-demand platform for homeowners who need a new roof.
18	Snapflat (Hong Kong)	2017	N/A	SnapFlat pays tenants 15% of a month's rent when they move out if they open the door for the viewings to help finding the next tenant.
19	Tower360 (Germany)	2017	-	TOWER360 is a Big Data Platform dedicated to Commercial Real Estate (CRE) providing real time and data driven insights to Asset Managers and Landlords.
20	Betterview (U.S.)	2014	4	Betterview is a platform for drone-based property inspections to help decision-makers who want to reduce risk, cost, and waste.

Source: Crunchbase, as of February 27, 2018

Printed in Great Britain
by Amazon